# Young Folks' Words of I

## The Sweet Stories of God's Word in the Language of Childhood

Josephine Pollard

(Contributor: John Henry Barrows, David Swing)

**Alpha Editions**

This edition published in 2024

ISBN : 9789362999306

Design and Setting By
**Alpha Editions**
www.alphaedis.com
Email - info@alphaedis.com

As per information held with us this book is in Public Domain.
This book is a reproduction of an important historical work. Alpha Editions uses the best technology to reproduce historical work in the same manner it was first published to preserve its original nature. Any marks or number seen are left intentionally to preserve its true form.

# PREFACE.

The word Bible is from the Greek, and means THE BOOK. It is made up of several small books, and when bound in two parts is known as the Old Testament and the New Testament. A Testament is a will; and the Bible is God's will made for man's good, and for his guide through life. The Old Testament tells of God's love and care for the Jews, and His thought of Christ can be traced through all its pages. There is a good deal in the Bible that a child cannot understand, and the queer names make it very hard reading.

It has been the Author's aim to tell the story simply, and in Bible language, so that the little ones can read it themselves, and learn to love and prize it as the best of all books.

J. P.

# INTRODUCTION.

## By Rev. William Henry Milburn, D. D.

NO man of his time filled a larger space in the public eye of this country than John Randolph of Roanoke. His eccentricities, audacity and brilliancy,—his pride of birth and race, fearlessness and self-assertion,—his incisive and trenchant speeches set off with sparkling wit, keen satire, fierce invective, clothed in perfect English, and uttered with the style of a master, his sharp criticisms of the faults and short-comings of his fellow-Congressmen, which gained for him the title, "schoolmaster of Congress," together with his political consistency and fitfulness of temper, invested all his movements and sayings with a peculiar charm for the people. In his earliest years he had been carefully taught by his beautiful mother, the Creed, the Lord's Prayer, the Ten Commandments, and many parts of God's Word, until he had them by heart, and yet, in his haughty youth and early manhood he strove to set at naught these teachings: furnished himself with a "whole body of infidelity," as he styled his collection of the writings of Voltaire and other French authors, as well as British, who strove to abolish the Bible, and for many years it seemed at once his pride and delight to wield the weapons drawn from these arsenals against the truths which make men wise unto Eternal Life, and to jeer with flout and scoff at all he had learned from his mother's lips. But later on he confessed, with heart-breaking sobs and bitter tears, that with all his arrogance and insolence, his stern resolve to become and continue a Deist, he had never been able to put aside for a single day or night the lessons taught him by his mother, and that the hallowed forms of sound words, learned on her lap or at her knee, had dwelt with him, and were ever sounding in his ears, to admonish, counsel and reprove. There have been few more pathetic scenes than that in which Randolph came to die; a gaunt old man, old before his time; worn out by misery, shrivelled and haggard, sitting upright in his bed, covered by a blanket, even his head enveloped and his hat on top of it; unutterable despair looking out at his eyes, his pinched lips and squeaking voice uttering, "Let me see it; get a dictionary; find me the word Remorse." A dictionary could not be found. "Write it; I must see it," he almost shrieked with failing voice. The word was written on his visiting card below his name; he demanded that it should be written above as well. The card was handed to him. "Remorse, John Randolph of Roanoke, Remorse." With horror in his face and that card in his hand, his eyes staring at the word, he breathed his last. From that mournful death-bed seemed to come floating the solemn words, "Take fast hold of instruction; keep her; let her not go, for she is thy life," and "He that sinneth against wisdom wrongeth his own soul."

Long centuries ago, a young man of aristocratic birth, handsome person, polished manners, brilliant and highly cultivated intellect, was walking, on a day in the reign of the Emperor Julian, by the bank of the river Orontes, not far from the stately city of Antioch, the Paris of that age,—and saw something floating in the stream. The branch of a tree enabled him to drag it ashore; it proved to be a copy of the sacred Scriptures; Julian, the mad master of the world, had issued an edict, annexed to which were heavy penalties, that all copies of that book should be destroyed. The young man who drew the manuscript to shore had been taught the lessons of that volume from a child, by his pious mother, Anthusa; but he had thrown off the yoke of his mother's faith; had become a devotee of heathen philosophy, poetry and rhetoric, and at the same time steeped himself in the licentious pleasures and dissipations of the Grove of Daphne, the Hippodrome and Theatre, and resolved that "the man Christ Jesus should not reign over him." He opened the parchment, some words on the page caught his eye; they were familiar, yet shone with a new light and were armed with irresistible power: he read on; his mother's prayers were answered; he embraced the truth, bowed his neck to the yoke he had foresworn, and the volume he rescued from the flood became a treasure-trove for the world,—through fifteen centuries alike in the east and west,—that man has been known as St. John Chrysostom, the "Mouth of Gold," one of the most saintly and eloquent preachers, whose life, genius, sufferings and death for conscience's sake adorned the history of mankind.

Not far from the same time, a young man bathed in tears lay writhing in agony under a fig tree in the garden of his house at Milan. His devout mother, Monica, in their Numidian home, had taught him the way of life written in God's Word; but as he grew to manhood he strove to shake off the influence and authority of her instruction; became a libertine, reached forth to grasp the crown of heathen eloquence and learning, and for more than ten years wrought steadily to undo the sacred work his mother had performed for him as a child. But the lesson she had taught him lay deeper than his surging passions, imperious intellect, and haughty will, and because of their power over him he could find no rest night or day. He journeyed to Carthage, Rome, Milan, the chief cities of the western world, to study art and eloquence, to drench his soul with the pleasures of sense and lay the ghost of his disquiet; but in vain. In his anguish under the fig tree he heard, or seemed to hear, again and again, "Take it up and read, Take it up and read." Springing to his feet, he ran to a friend near by who was reading the Word. Seizing the volume, his eyes rested on the words, "Let us walk honestly as in the day; not in rioting and drunkenness, not in chambering and wantonness, not in strife and envying. But put ye on the Lord Jesus Christ and make not provisions for the flesh, to fulfill the lusts thereof." The birth-pangs of his conversion were ended; he found peace in believing; and that incident makes an era in the history of the world, for that man was none other than Saint Augustine, the influence of whose writings has swayed with more might than that of an imperial sceptre the destinies of western Christendom for ages. "Therefore, whosoever heareth these sayings of mine and doeth them," saith the Lord, "I will liken him unto a wise man which built his house upon a rock; and the rain descended, and the floods came, and the winds blew and beat upon that house; and it fell not, for it was founded upon a rock. And every one that heareth these sayings of mine, and doeth them not, shall be likened unto a foolish man which built his house upon the sand; and the rains descended, and the floods came, and the winds blew and beat upon that house and it fell, and great was the fall of it." Woe to Randolph! he heard and would not, and his house fell, and great was the fall of it. Mankind with one voice calls Augustine and Chrysostom blessed; they heard, obeyed, and their houses stand forever; they were built upon the rock. "Their Rock is not as our Rock, our enemies themselves being judges" was the boast of Israel at an early day. With how much fuller emphasis may Christendom utter it to-day. Compare India with Britain, China with the United States, and after all other forces are measured and allowed, it will be found that the significant and self-renewing causes for the superiority of the western nations over the eastern are the presence, authority and influence of the Old and New Testament. "And he shewed me a pure river of water of life clear as crystal proceeding out of the throne of God and of the Lamb. In the midst of the street of it, and on either side of the river, was there the tree of life, which bare twelve manner of fruits and yielded her fruit every month; and the leaves of the tree were for the healing of the nations."

In this beautiful book, Miss Pollard, with admirable tact and skill, has made a path by which the children may draw near to that river and drink of the water of life; and the artists whose genius has been laid under such effective contribution by the liberality of the publisher, will help the little ones to gather the leaves and pluck the fruit of that tree.

Every home in the land blessed by the presence of boys and girls will be illumined and enriched by this volume; every mother who strives to train her children "in the nurture and admonition of the Lord" will be signally helped by its ministry.

The letter-press will quicken the understanding and attune the ear, and the treasures of art contained in these pages will arouse the imagination and stimulate the memory of the young to lay hold upon and receive all that is contained in "the one Book—" "Oldest Choral melody as of the heart of mankind; soft and great as the summer midnight, as the world with the seas and stars."

No man's education can be complete, no human life can have its full store of flowers and fruits, which is not begun, continued and ended in the ever deepening study and love of the articulate word of God.

I cannot better close this introduction than with this remarkable passage, modified to suit my purpose. "Who will say that the uncommon beauty and marvelous English of the household Bible is not the stronghold and safeguard of the literary taste and culture of this country as well as its character. It lives like a music that can never be forgotten, like the sound of church bells which the reader hardly knows how he can forego. Its felicities often seem to be almost things rather than mere words. It is part of the national mind, and the anchor of national seriousness. The memory of the dead passes into it. The potent traditions of childhood are stereotyped into its phrases. The power of all the man's griefs and trials are hidden beneath its words. It is the representative of his best moments; and all that there has been about him of soft and gentle and pure and penitent and good, speaks to him forever out of his English Bible. It is his sacred thing, which doubt has never dimmed and controversy never soiled. It has been to him all along as the silent, yet oh, how intelligible! voice of his guardian angel, and in the length and breadth of the land there is not a Christian, with one spark of religiousness about him, whose spiritual Biography is not in his Saxon Bible."

WASHINGTON, April, 1889.

# THE CHILD AND THE BIBLE.

### By Prof. David Swing.

THAT reading and study are very imperfect which do not bring to all our young people a knowledge of the general contents of the Bible. The Old and New Testaments contain the best moral and religious thought and belief of two important epochs in man's history—the Hebrew and Christian periods. It contains the history, the wisdom, the morality, the piety and the hope of that part of the human race that made religion the chief aim of the nation and the individual. The Hebrew people was set apart for the special task of carrying forward the idea of God. That race gradually separated the real Creator from the many false divinities of the barbarian tribes and slowly built up that conception of Deity which is seen set forth in the Book of Job and in the twenty-third and nineteenth Psalms. The Book of Job and the Psalms of David are the grand autumnal fruitage of that vineyard of worship in which Enoch and Abraham were toilers in the early springtime of our world.

No such advance toward the true God would have taken place had the Mosaic race moved out of Egypt only to found a State which might build elsewhere duplicates of the pyramids of the Nile, or a State which, like Babylonia, might live only for luxury, or which, like Greece, might live only for the fine arts, or which, like Rome, might find a reason of being in wars of conquest. Divinely led, the Hebrew people migrated from Egypt that beyond the Red Sea and the Jordan they might found a republic or empire for the study and founding of the true religion. Israel stands as the wonder of the past, the only nation in all history that elected God for its king and went up into a high mountain so as to deduce its laws from the thunder and storm and from the sunlight and peace of His presence. With what success it achieved its task may be learned from reading the meditations in Job and the Psalms, and from the lofty rhapsodies of Isaiah and Malachi. When to the sacred records of that long day and night of toil and progress are added the coming of the divine Christ and the moral phenomena of the first Christian century, a book is composed at which to scoff is a proof of a weak or a wicked mind, and in which to read often and thoughtfully is evidence of a willingness to seek after the living God and to find the best answers to the many problems of life and death.

Much that is valuable in these two testaments is recorded in events or in parables, and for all young minds and for nearly all older intellects, the doctrines, the alarms, the benedictions, the promises, the hopes are treasured up in incidents which might be thrown upon canvas or carved out of marble. Faith is seen in the picture of Abraham; patriotism, courage, honor, piety in Moses; justice in the story of Lot's wife; eternal friendship in Ruth; reckless ambition in Absalom; resignation in Job; faithfulness in Daniel; while in the New Testament the pictures offered in the Christ, the Marys, the Johns and St. Paul have been too many and too great for art to equal.

These incidents and persons of the Bible form in the mind of the one who knows them a perfect treasure-house filled with the gems of true religion. When that gifted writer who composed the hymn "Nearer my God to Thee" sat down to her task, what an imperfection would have marked her poem had she not known of Jacob's stony pillow and beautiful dream!

Though like a wanderer,
The sun gone down,
Darkness be over me,
My rest a stone.

And the two following stanzas would have been wanting; nor is it probable that the writer, although a woman most gifted, could have found in all literature any compensation for her loss and our loss. In the "Battle-Hymn of the Republic," the eloquent writer shows in her first line her memory of Simeon, and through his eyes she looked and said: "Mine eyes have seen the glory of the coming of the Lord," and in the last verse, back comes one of the most beautiful incidents in the New Testament: "In the beauty of the lilies, Christ was born across the sea."

Thus have thousands of years, in all, acted as the great time-space for attaching the Hebrew and Christian mind and heart to the persons and incidents found in the Holy Scriptures. Not to know all these Heaven-sent emblems of virtue, wisdom, piety and salvation is not only not to be a Christian, but it is to stand afar off from the honor of even a common education and the most needful culture.

For the youth of our country Josephine Pollard, a wonderful friend of all those who are living their early years, and as good a writer as she is a friend, has detached from the Bible this volume of historic incidents, and while they make a continuous record of the old and the new dispensations, they are separated from that which is too abstract to detain and impress the youngest readers. To these interesting events she has made the engraver add his art, and the picture of the pencil comes to help the picture more hidden in the words. While Christ is speaking of the "lost sheep" the picture reveals the lonely mountains and the lamb missed from the flock. While the great Teacher is speaking of the foolish virgins, the picture appears of the thoughtless ones attempting in vain to find oil for their lamps. Thus the pictures of history combine with the suggestive sketches of the artist and engraver, to make, indeed, a Bible for Young People. The authoress came to her task with rare fitness, and while the young folks are reading her volume they will find not only the religious truths they all need, but they will also find the simplicity and power of their own English language.

# AN ADDRESS TO CHILDREN.

## BY JOHN H. BARROWS, D.D.

### THE BIBLE THE BOOK FOR THE YOUNG.

GOD once said: "And thou shalt teach them diligently to thy children." The whole Bible, Old Testament and New, was meant to be taught to the boys and girls all over the world. When I was in Egypt, fifteen years ago, I lay one beautiful moonlight night on the white sand of an island in the river Nile. It was an island away up near the equator, and as I lay there I saw beautiful trees with their long, leafy branches above me; I saw green fields reaching out on either side; I heard the old river Nile rippling over the stones in its bed; and I thought of the rich fields of cotton and wheat and sugar-cane and of the thousands of palm trees which I had seen along the river, and of all the people who had gotten their bread from the waters of the Nile, which, covering the sand of the desert, make it fertile and fruitful, and I blessed God for the Nile. Where does it come from? You have learned that the Nile springs from the snows of very high mountains away up in Abyssinia, and from two immense lakes in the center of Africa, and it carries the waters from these mountains and lakes down through Egypt, and turns a desert into a garden.

But there is another river more wonderful than the river of old Egypt. It flows down from God out of heaven, and flows over this world, and brings with it all that is beautiful and healthful and good. The waters of this river are carried off in little canals, and are brought into the homes and churches and Sunday-schools; and wherever they go tend to make lives good and happy. Little children love this River of God, and dip their cups into it and drink, and there is a voice speaking in their ears and saying: "Whosoever will, let him take of the water of life freely." There are some people who have traveled round the world and seen many very interesting lands and strange and curious people—white men, red men, black men, copper-colored men, yellow men, but they will tell you that they never saw men where the children were happy, where the homes were happy, and where people were trying to do each other good, unless this River of God went there first. This beautiful river that is doing so much for all who live on its banks,—it is the Bible, the Word of God, which tells us about Himself and about ourselves, which speaks to us of a Savior and of the life after death.

Some years ago a black prince in Africa sent a messenger to Queen Victoria, a man who was to ask her what was the reason that England was so rich and prosperous; and she sent back to this African savage something that told the whole story. What do you suppose it was? Not a rifle, not a sword, not a steam-engine, not a plow, not a sewing-machine, but a copy of the Bible. Let me tell you *five* things about this book, and if you know how to spell the word Bible you will find them easy to remember—B-I-B-L-E.

First, then, the Bible is a *beautiful* book. I do not mean as to its shape and color. It may be very lovely or it may be very plain, as it looks to your eye. I have seen Bibles that you could buy for a sixpence, and I have a New Testament that I bought for a penny. I have seen Bibles which were copied with a pen and filled with pictures on which men labored for years, and which you couldn't buy for a thousand dollars. When I say that the Bible is a beautiful book, I mean that it is full of beautiful thoughts and beautiful pictures and beautiful stories that speak to our minds. God often talks with children through pictures. You love things that speak to you through the eye, like flowers and birds, and your dear mother's face. Just think of some of the pictures God has given us in this Book.

I see, with my mind's eye, a garden, large, fair, with great trees and beautiful walks, pure, clear streams with lovely flowers, with animals playing about, with two trees that were set apart from the rest, one called the Tree of Life and the other the Tree of the Knowledge of Good and Evil. I see a man in this garden, and animals passing before him and hear him giving them names. Now I see a city with twelve gates, each gate a pearl. The city has walls made of twelve kinds of jewels, and the streets are of pure gold, and there is no temple in the city and no sun, but it is very glorious and wonderful. I see a beautiful River and a glorious Sea, and a great multitude of shining ones with harps in their hands, and I see a throne and One that sits thereon, more lovely and beautiful and mighty and glorious than any words can say.

The little three-year-old boy before he can read, loves to take his picture book and see things that are to him very wonderful, and when he gets a little older he loves to take a box of paints and a brush and color the pictures in some of his books. The first book I ever colored was full of Bible pictures. There was the picture of a man on the top of a hill with his son laid on a heap of stones. The father's face was sad, and the old man was lifting a knife in his hand; and there was a sheep caught in a bush near by; and there was the figure of an angel in the sky. Then there was the picture of a young man lying on the ground, with stones under his head for a pillow, and a stairway or ladder reaching up to the heavens above, with angels going up and down. There was the picture of a boy whose father gave him a coat of many colors, and how I liked to daub on the red and yellow and blue paint, and I am afraid I took a pin and punched out the eyes in the pictures of the brothers of this boy—those brothers who, as you remember, cast him into a dry well and afterward sold him as a slave. There was a picture of a little boy lying in a little boat which was among the tall grasses of a river. There was the picture of a great tent in the desert, with altars on which fire was burning, and a great pillar of cloud resting down on it in the midst of the tent. And then far over in the book was the picture of the best Man who ever lived, taking little children in His arms, putting His hands on them and blessing them.

The Bible is a beautiful book for a great many reasons that I can't speak of now. Its beauty is not like that of an apple blossom, which soon fades away. It grows more and more lovely as you grow older. I like to see a little child reading with happy face from this book which tells of God's love; but it is lovelier still to see the old grandmother, who loved the Bible in childhood, putting on her spectacles and reading these words of David: "Oh, how I love thy law! It is my meditation all the day. How sweet are thy words to my taste, yea, sweeter than honey to my mouth!" Two of the most beautiful things that we ever see are gold and honey—gold, bright shining, and the honey which looks like liquid gold, shut up in little boxes of pearl. Now I am going to end what I have to say about the Bible as beautiful, by telling you what David said of the words of the Lord that are found in this book: "More to be desired are they than gold, yea, than much fine gold; sweeter also than honey and the honey comb."

But the Bible is not only a beautiful book for children, but it is an *interesting* book. You like to read it and hear it, partly because it tells so much about children, boys and girls like you. You read in this book about two brothers, one of whom loved God, and the other did not love his brother, and slew him because his own deeds were evil and his brother's righteous. You read about a little girl who was taken off in a certain war, and became a servant for the wife of a great general. He was a leper, and this little girl, believing in God and in God's prophet, Elisha, told her mistress that the prophet in Israel could heal her master of his awful disease. You read the story of a little boy whose mother gave him early to the Lord, and who went to live with an old man in a great tent, which was God's house, and who heard the voice of the Lord calling to him in the night. Did you never hear God's voice speaking to your heart, and do you always answer as did this boy in the tabernacle at Shiloh: "Speak, Lord, for thy servant heareth"?

And in this Book you have read of four boys in the court of the great king of Babylon who would not defile themselves with the rich meats and the fiery wines, and who formed a boys' temperance society in the court of the king, and who rose to high honor and great fame. Above all, you read of the perfect Child who was obedient to his earthly father and mother, and who did the will of his Heavenly Father, and who grew into the bravest, noblest, truest, most manly man that ever lived, and who died for us all—that Man whose words are, I think, the first words of the Bible that you learned by heart. I have heard of a little girl who lived where the Bible is not permitted to be read by the children. But she had a present of the good Book from her Sunday School teacher. It was discovered that she had this book; it was snatched from her and thrown into the fire. She watched it burn, while the tears rolled down her cheeks, and turning sadly away, said: "Thank God, there are fourteen chapters of the Gospel of John which they can't burn up, for I have committed them to memory."

The Bible interests you because it is full of *wonderful* things. It tells of a wonderful God who doeth marvelous things for His people. It tells of the flood which swept away the wicked world; of the plagues which fell on wicked Egypt; of the march of two millions of people through the Red Sea which God divided; it tells you of the wonderful life of the children of Israel in the desert, with God's hand feeding them with the birds and the bread; it leads you to the foot of a great mountain, on which God came down in a chariot of fire, while the thunders roared and the trumpet blown by some mighty angel sounded loud and long, and the mountain shook and smoked like a great furnace, and all the people trembled while God gave the law which begins: "I am the Lord that brought thee out of Egypt. Thou shalt have no other gods before me."

This Bible has more wonderful things than you will find anywhere else. It tells of great battles, of the sun and moon standing still, of cities falling down at the blowing of trumpets; of fire descending from heaven; it tells of shipwrecks and storms, and cruel kings, and men willing to die for the name of Jesus. It tells of God's wonderful love, and how the Son of God came from heaven to earth and died for us on the Cross and rose from the grave. And the best thing, children, about all these Bible wonders, is this, that they are true. A wonderful God doeth wonderful things. This is a wonderful world we live in. You children know it and feel it, and some older people have got to become much wiser than they now are to be as wise as you are. Is not the Bible an interesting Book? My children will listen longer to the story of the Bible than anything else. And as you grow older, if you will only keep on studying the Bible, it will keep its interest till you die.

Children who live in cities love to ride, in summer, in the parks and see the wonderful figures which the gardeners have made with their plants and flowers, the stars and stripes, an elephant, the ball-player, a giraffe, a sun-dial, a calendar, an obelisk, sphinxes, and so forth. Now, this book is a great garden on which God has made figures that will last as long as the world lasts. There is Adam, with his face dark and sorrowful because he had sinned; there is Abel, looking up to that heaven which he, first of all men, entered; there is Noah, a preacher of righteousness, who preached many years without converting a soul, but kept on believing God; there is Abraham with a staff in his hand; there is Moses holding the wondrous rod and the book of the law; there is David with his harp; there is Paul, going forth to preach Christ;

there is John, looking into heaven. The children who have the Bible taught them will find great interest in these figures. But the greatest interest in the Bible is this, that it is a sign-board pointing us to our Father's house in Heaven.

Now, I come to the third letter. The B-I-*B*-L-E—is not only a Beautiful book, and an Interesting book, but it is a Blessed book. That is, it makes people happy and good, good and happy. A poor man comes from England to Chicago with his wife and three children, expecting to get work and to make him a lovely home. But he fails to get work and he has to sell many things to get bread for his family. At last he is in despair, but a good man comes to his house, learns of his need, gives him bread and gets him work; and that night the Englishman says to his wife, "Wasn't he a blessed man to help us at this time?" But in a few days the baby of the house is taken sick and soon dies, and the good man comes again and advances money to pay for the funeral of the dear little child; and they say, "Blessed man!" again. But that night, when all is over, and the baby is laid to sleep in the cemetery, the poor man takes down the Bible and reads to his wife of Christ's love to children, and of the beautiful world beyond, where there is no more crying and death, and the wife says, "Oh, isn't that a blessed Book!"

*Blessed* Book. So the mother thinks whose boy has gone off to school or to sea. How careful she was to put a copy of the Bible in his hands and to get from him the promise to read it every day. She knows perfectly well that no great harm can come to him, if he reads and obeys what is written in the Word of God. I know a young lady who was very much distressed when in Paris several years ago because her hand-bag, a little portmanteau, had been lost. And when, after much hunting, it was found, she confessed that what distressed her most of all in the thought of losing her hand-bag was this, that it contained the little Bible which had been given to her when a child and which she had made her daily companion ever since. I hope that each of you owns a Bible which, the gift of a mother or of some dear friend, is growing more and more blessed to you as you go forward into your lives. There is much darkness in the future. You will have sorrows as well as joys. The clouds will gather. The shadows will sometimes descend and you will wonder where you are to walk, or what you are to do. But remember what David has said of this blessed Book: "Thy word is a lamp to my feet and a guide to my path."

Now, we come to the fourth letter, B-I-B-*L*-E. Beautiful, Interesting, Blessed, L, Life-giving. This is something better than anything we have yet said to you about the Bible. It gives life to those who are dead. You have seen a patch of ground early in the spring on which nothing was growing. But the rain falls, and the warm sunshine pours down, and the seeds in that soil burst into life and spring up and cover the earth with living plants and flowers. And so God's Word brings its dew and sunshine on our cold, dead hearts, and the flowers of love, hope, peace and joy spring up. The Bible is like bread, like the manna which came to the children of Israel in the desert. It feeds our souls. It gives us life. How does it give us life? It teaches us about God and his great love in Jesus, and when we come to get from Him the forgiveness of our sins, when we come to know God and love God and trust in God, we have life. "This is life eternal," said Jesus, "that they may know thee, the only true God, and Jesus Christ whom thou hast sent." Some of you are giving money to send this Book to the heathen people. Where this Book goes it gives life like bread sent to people who are starving.

But why do we need the Bible to know about God? Do not the stars and the sun and the earth tell us that there must be a God who made all these wonderful things and rules them? Yes, they tell us that God is powerful, that He is very great, but they do not tell us that he loves us poor sinners. The Egyptians believed in God; yes, in many gods. They were, as we know, a very wise and learned people. And yet this people Moses found bowing down and worshiping cats and crocodiles and beetles. They did not know the one God who led His people, and who said, "Thou shalt have no other gods before me," and who is not only holy, but merciful, forgiving our sins. Suppose that you were on an ocean steamer way out at sea, and she was sinking into the waves. To what or to whom would you pray? You wouldn't pray to the waves. They would not have mercy on you. You wouldn't pray to the stars. They wouldn't have mercy on you. You would pray to the God who is revealed in this Book, the God and Father of our Lord Jesus Christ, who has said that nothing can take us from His love, neither life nor death, land nor ocean, nothing can separate us from His love.

Children, this Book tells us one thing which all need to learn, and that is, how we may gain life eternal, how we may escape from death. This Book is the story of God's love. It is the story of Jesus, our Savior. He that has Christ in his heart has life. "I am the resurrection and the life," said Jesus; "I am the way, the truth and the life." If this Book does not lead you to Christ, you have failed to get from it what God gave it for. David said of the Bible: "The law of the Lord is perfect, converting the soul."

We come now to the fifth letter, B-I-B-L-*E*—Everlasting. The Bible is Beautiful, Interesting, Blessed, Life-giving, and Everlasting. It is something that does not wear out. "The word of the Lord endureth forever." Children's clothes wear out, as you well know. Your play-things break; your shoes don't last; your books get torn; these bodies die; but the Bible lasts. It was good in David's time. It was good when Christ was a child, and He read it. It was good in Paul's time, and he added to it. It was good when Martin Luther translated it into the German language, and William Tyndale translated it into English. It lasts the way an oak tree lasts, that grows bigger and bigger and sends out little shoots that grow into other oaks and make a mighty forest. This Bible is now speaking to men in nearly three hundred different languages. It is going to be the one Book of the world. A hundred years ago a famous infidel in France, named Voltaire, foolishly published his opinion that the religion of the Bible would soon die out, but to-day men are using Voltaire's printing-press in Geneva to publish this grand old Book. Here is something, children, that is going to last. You can stand on it safely. God is in it. When the little girl whose father was an infidel and whose mother was a Christian was dying, and she said to her father, "Shall I hold to your principles, father, or shall I turn now to my mother's God?" the father said: "Believe in your mother's God."

Just before beginning a great battle on the sea, you remember that Admiral Nelson hung out a flag with these words for all to see: "England expects every man to do his duty." And so our great General, the Captain of our salvation, expects that every boy trained up in a Christian church will do his duty. He expects that you will take this Beautiful, Interesting, Blessed, Life-giving and Eternal book and make it your guide, your compass, your rudder, your chart on the great ocean of life. He expects that you will be true men and women, honest, pure, obedient to God, loving your country and all the world. He expects that you will be faithful to duty, that you will be clean in body and in lips and mouth and eyes and heart. He expects to meet you and welcome you all in glory above.

A passenger on one of our ocean steamers found an old friend in the captain. They talked about one of their old classmates in school. Said the passenger: "I could never understand why Will did not succeed. He left college well educated, full of life and health, well-to-do. He gave up the ministry which he had intended to enter, having fallen in with some free-thinking fellows. He studied law, but gave that up and went to farming. He became a skeptic. He left his wife and farming and became a gold-seeker in California. He left this and went to Idaho. He had lost everything, and supported himself by odd jobs. I knew him there. He was not a drunkard or a gambler, but he had never succeeded. He tried something new several times a year. He was now almost mad in his opposition to the religion of the Bible. Soon he died, bitterly rebelling against God. It is wonderful that such a man should ever have come to such an end."

The captain was silent for a while, but at last said: "Old sailors have a superstition that there are phantom ships (that is, ghosts of ships) which cross the sea. I saw a vessel once that showed me how this idea may have sprung up. It was a full-rigged bark, driving under full sail. There was no one on board. Some disease may have broken out, and all the sailors had left. I could not capture her, though I tried. Several months later I passed her again. Her topmast was gone; her sails were in rags; the wind drove her where it would. A year later she came in sight one stormy winter night. She was a shattered hulk and went down at last in the darkness and storm. She was a good ship at first, but," added the captain, "she had lost her rudder." Boys and girls, young men and women, I pray you, on this voyage of life, not to lose the rudder by which, in the storm, you may hold the ship true to the harbor.

---

# HISTORY OF THE OLD TESTAMENT.

## CHAPTER I.

### GOD MADE THE WORLD.

FAR back in the past, more years than you could think or count, God made the world. It did not look at first as it does now, for there was no live thing on it, no men, beasts, or birds, not a bush, tree or plant, but all was dark and drear.

Then God said, Let there be light! And the light came. And God saw the light, and it pleased him, and he gave it the name of Day. And when the day was gone, and the dark came back to stay for a while, he gave the dark spell the name of Night. And God did these things on the first day.

The next day God made the clouds, and the sky in which they were to move; and he gave the sky a name; he called it Heav-en.

Then he drove the wa-ters to one place where they were both deep and wide, and he called the wa-ters Seas, and to the dry land he gave the name of Earth. And God made the grass to grow up out of the earth, and the trees and shrubs that have fruit on them. And the grass and the shrubs and the trees were to bear seeds, so that when these seeds were put in-to the ground more grass and trees and shrubs would grow there. God did these things on the third day.

And God put two great lights in the sky, the Sun to shine by day, and the Moon to shine by night; and he made the stars, and put each one in its place. And these things he did on the fourth day.

And he made the great whales, and all the fish that live in the sea, and the birds that swim on it, as well as those that fly through the air, and make their nests in the deep woods. And these things God did on the fifth day.

God made the beasts: those that are wild and live in the deep, dark woods, far from the homes of men; and those that are tame and of use to men, and live where men live—such as the horse, the cow, the ox and the sheep. And he made the things that creep on the ground, and flies and bugs that course through the air.

**AD-AM AND EVE DRIV-EN FROM PAR-A-DISE.**

And then God made Man, and told him that he should rule the fish of the sea, the birds of the air, and all else that lived on the earth. And he told man that the fruit which grew on the trees and shrubs should be his food, while the beasts were to feed on the leaves, and on the grass that was spread out on the earth. These things were done on the sixth day.

The next day God did no work at all, but made it a day of rest.

God made man out of the dust of the earth, and breathed in him till the man breathed and moved, and showed signs of life. Then God made a gar-den for man to live in, where all sorts of trees grew that were nice to look at, and that bore fruit good to eat. And this place was called E-den. And through it flowed a large stream that kept the earth moist.

And God took Ad-am, the man he had made, and put him in the gar-den, and told him to take care of it. He told him he might eat of the fruit that grew on all the trees but one. God said he must not eat of that tree, for if he did he would be sure to die. And all the birds and beasts came to A-dam, that he might give them their names. And the names he gave them are those by which they are known to this day.

And God saw it was not good for man to be a-lone; he should have some one to be with him and help him. So he had a deep sleep fall on Ad-am, and while he slept God took out of his side a bone, and out of this bone he made a wo-man. Then he brought this wo-man he had made to Ad-am, and she was his wife.

Now there was in this gar-den of E-den a great big snake. And this snake spoke to the wo-man—as Sa-tan speaks to us—to tempt her to sin.

The snake said: Has God told you not to eat of all the trees in the gar-den?

And the wo-man said that they might eat of all but one; if they ate of that or touched it they would be sure to die. The snake told them they should not die, and that God did not wish them to eat of it for fear they would grow wise, and know more than he thought was good for them.

The wo-man heard what the snake said, and when she saw that the tree was nice to look at and the fruit seemed good to eat, she gave no thought to what God had said, but took some of the fruit and ate of it; she gave some to the man, Ad-am, and he did eat.

In a short time they heard a voice, and knew that God spoke to them. Yet they did not come near him when they heard his voice, but ran and tried to hide from him.

But God spoke once more, and said to the man, Where art thou?

And Ad-am said, I heard thy voice, and my fear was so great that I hid from thee.

And God said, Did'st thou eat of the tree I told thee not to eat of?

And the man said, She whom thou dids't give me to be with me brought me some of the fruit, and I did eat.

And God said to the man's wife, What is this that thou hast done?

And she told God what the snake had said, and how she came to eat of the fruit, and God was wroth with them all. He said the snake should crawl on the ground and eat dust all the days of its life; and he told the wife she should know what it was to be sick and sad, and should have much grief and care.

And God drove the man and his wife out of E-den, and would let them live no more in that fair place. And he sent an-gels to keep watch, and a sword of fire that would turn in all ways, so that the two whom God for their sins drove out of E-den could not get back to the home they had lost.

And God told Ad-am that as he had paid heed to what his wife said, and did eat of the tree which the Lord had told him not to eat of, the ground should bear no more fruit for him by it-self, as it had done up to this time, and Ad-am would have to work hard all his life to raise food to eat, and when he died he would go back to the dust out of which he was made.

But God told Ad-am and his wife that there was a way by which their souls might live on high when their flesh was laid in the ground. He said he would send One from the sky who would give his life for theirs: that is, he would be put to death for their sins. Then if they would turn from their sins, and give their hearts to the One who was to save them, God would not turn his face from them, but when they died they would have a home with him, and have no thought of sin.

So Ad-am went forth to till the land, and he gave his wife the name of Eve. And they made coats out of the skins of beasts.

**CAIN AND A-BEL OF-FER-ING SAC-RI-FI-CES TO GOD.**

Ad-am and his wife had two sons: Cain and A-bel. When they grew up to be men, Cain, who was the first-born, took care of a farm; A-bel kept a flock of sheep.

They both had bad hearts, and at times would be led in-to sin, just as Ad-am and his wife had been. But when A-bel did wrong he was grieved, and sought to make peace with God. One day he brought a lamb from his flock, and killed it, and burnt it on a heap of stones. And the smoke went up on high.

This act of A-bel's pleased God, for it was the sign that a Lamb was to be sent to the world to save men from their sins.

But Cain kept on in his sins, and paid his vows to God not with a lamb, but with fruit or grain out of the field. This did not please God, and the smoke went not up on high. When Cain saw this he was in a rage, and showed by his looks that he was wroth with God. Yet God spoke to him in a kind voice, and said, Why art thou wroth? and why art thou so cast down?

If Cain did right God told him he would be pleased with his gift; but if he did not do right, the fault was his own.

Then Cain was wroth with A-bel, for he saw that God was pleased with A-bel's gift and not with his. And one day when both of them were out in the field he rose up and slew A-bel, and the blood ran out of A-bel's wounds and sank deep in the ground.

As soon as this deed was done, God spoke to Cain, and said: Where is A-bel?

Cain said, I know not. He is not in my care. Then God, who had seen the crime, and knew just how bad his heart was, said to Cain: What hast thou done? The voice of A-bel's blood cries to me from out the ground.

And God told Cain that for his great sin he should move from place to place, as one who was in fear of his life, and had no home to stay in. And if he should plant aught in the field to bear food, it should not grow well. Weeds would come up and choke it, or it would bear leaves and no fruit, so that Cain would not have much to eat.

## THE DEATH OF A-BEL.

And Cain said if God drove him here and there on the face of the earth, and would not take care of him, all those who met him would want to kill him.

But God said the man who hurt Cain would have a worse fate. God set a mark on Cain; what kind of a mark it was we are not told, but those who saw it would know it was Cain, and it would bring to their minds that God had said no man should kill him.

Ad-am lived to be an old, old man, and had a large flock of chil-dren, who grew up and were wed, and they went off and made homes, and day by day were folks born in-to the world. When Ad-am died he was laid in the ground and went back to dust, as God had said he should when he went out of E-den.

One of the men who lived in those days was named E-noch. It is said of him that he walked with God. That means that he loved God, and thought of him, and kept near him all the time, and did his best to please him.

And E-noch did not die, but God took him up to be with him while he still lived, just as if he were to take up one of us.

And E-noch had a son whose name was Me-thu-se-lah, who died at a great old age. In those times men lived more years than they do now, but in all the years since the world was made no man has been known to live to be as old as Me-thu-se-lah.

# CHAPTER II.

## THE GREAT FLOOD; AND A GREAT TOWER.

IN the course of time, when there came to be more folks in the world, they grew fond of sin. They did not love God, or try to please him. And God was wroth with them, and said he would send a flood that would drown the world, and there should not be any dry land left for men, beasts, or birds to live on.

But though most of the folks at that time were as bad as they could be, there was one good man in their midst, and his name was No-ah.

**THE ARK.**

And God loved No-ah and told him what he meant to

do. And God bade No-ah build an ark. This was a boat. It was to be made large, with rooms in it, and a great door on its side. And it was to be quite high, and to have a roof on top.

And God told No-ah when the ark was done he and his sons and their wives should go in it.

And he told No-ah to take in with him two of each kind of bird and of beast, and of bug, and of things that crept, and to take care of them in the ark so long as the flood should be on the earth; for all that were not in the ark would be sure to be drowned.

So No-ah set out at once to build the ark; and it took him a great while to build it. When not at work on the ark, he would talk of God, and of his plan to send a flood to wash sin out of the world, and would urge the folks to give up their sins, and lead good lives. But they paid no heed to his words, and went from bad to worse all the time that No-ah was at work on the ark.

When it was done God told No-ah to come in-to the ark, for he saw he was a good man who had done his best to serve him, and to bring the birds and beasts with him. For in a few days he would send the rain on the earth, and all that was left on it would be drowned.

**THE ARK**

So No-ah did as God told him. And when he and his wife, and his three sons and their wives, and the birds and the beasts, both small and great, had passed through the great door of the ark, God shut them in.

At the end of a week the rain set in, and did not stop for more than a month. The rain seemed to pour out of the sky, and all the springs, the large and small streams, and the great seas, rose up and swept through the length and breadth of the land. They came to where the ark was, and went round and round it, and rose so high that the ark was borne from its place and set afloat on the great wide sea.

Then those who had paid no heed to No-ah, but had kept on in their sins, were in a sad plight. The flood had come, and they knew now that all that he had told them was true. How glad they would have been to go with him in the ark. But it was too late. They ran in wild haste to the tops of the hills in hopes to find there a safe place. But still the floods rose and rose till there was no place for them to go, and all those not in the ark were drowned, and there was not a bit of dry land in the whole wide world.

But God took care of No-ah, and those who were with him, and kept them safe till the floods went down. At the end of five months the sea had gone down so much that the ark stood high and dry on a mount known as Ar-a-rat. It stood there for at least two months, and at the end of that time the sea had gone down so that tops of high hills could be seen here and there.

And No-ah sent forth a ra-ven, and the bird flew this way and that, but came not back to the ark.

Then No-ah sent forth a dove, that he might find out if the ground was yet dry. And the dove flew here and there in search of green things, but found not a tree in sight, and naught but cold hard rock, and so she flew back to the ark and No-ah put out his hand and took her in.

At the end of a week No-ah sent out the dove once more, and at the close of the day she came back with a leaf in her mouth.

**THE RE-TURN OF THE DOVE.**

As soon as No-ah saw the leaf he knew that the waves had gone down or the dove could not have found it. And he knew that God had sent the dove back to him that he might know the ground would soon be dry.

In a few days he sent the dove out for the third time, but she did not come back; and No-ah was sure then that the ground was dry, and that God meant that for a sign that he should leave the ark in which he had been shut up so long.

And God spoke to No-ah and told him to come out of the ark, and to bring out all that had been in there with him. And No-ah did so, and he built up a heap of stones as A-bel had done, on which he laid beasts and birds, and burnt them, which was the way in which man gave thanks to God in those days.

And No-ah's heart was full of praise to God, who had kept him, and those who were near and dear to him, safe from the flood, while all the rest of the world was drowned.

And God told No-ah and his sons that they should rule on the earth, and might kill the beasts and use the flesh for food. Up to this time those who dwelt on the earth had lived on the fruits of trees and such things as grew out of the ground, and did not know the taste of meat.

And God told No-ah that he would send no more floods to drown the world as this one had done. And he gave No-ah a sign that he would keep his word, so that when No-ah saw it he would have no fear of a flood. And this sign was the rain-bow, which God set up in the sky as a bow of hope to No-ah and to all the world.

No-ah lived for years and years af-ter the flood, and died at a ripe old age.

The tribes of No-ah grew so fast that the world was quite well filled once more.

**NO-AH'S SAC-RI-FICE.**

And you would think they would have been glad to serve God, and to do right in his sight. But their hearts were full of sin, and they went on as those had done who were drowned in the flood.

**HE-BREWS, AND THEIR MODE OF TRAV-EL-ING.**

At this time all those who dwelt on the earth spoke but one tongue; that is, they used the same kind of speech.

Now these tribes did not stay in one spot all the time, but would pack up their tents and move from place to place as they chose.

And as they went to the east they came to a plain in the land of Shi-nar. And they said, Let us make brick and build a high tow-er that shall reach up to the sky. And let us make a name, so that when we go from this place it will be known what great men were here, and what great deeds they could do.

## BUILD-ING THE TOW-ER OF BA-BEL.

And they set to work to build it. God, who read their hearts, knew that sin was at work there, and that the tow-er they meant to build was not to serve him in, or to add to his praise. So he was not pleased with their work, and chose a strange way to stop them. He made them all at once speak in strange tongues. This one could not tell what that one said, and they made such a noise that it grew to be just a ba-bel of sound. And that is why it was called the tow-er of Ba-bel.

# CHAPTER III.

## ABRAHAM: THE MAN OF FAITH.

THERE dwelt in the land of Ur a man whose name was A-bra-ham. And in that land the men did not serve the true God, but had set up false gods to whom they paid their vows.

And God told A-bra-ham to leave his home and go to a land which he would show him. A-bra-ham did not know where the land was, but he had great faith, and knew that God would take care of him and bring him to the land he had told him of.

So A-bra-ham took Sa-rah, his wife, and his bro-ther's son, whose name was Lot, and they set out for the land which God had said he would show him.

A-bra-ham was a rich man, and so was Lot, and they had a great wealth of flocks, and of herds, and of tents. And they each had a large force of herds-men. And these herds-men were at strife.

And A-bra-ham told Lot it was best that they should part; and he said to him, Choose where thou shalt go. If thou wilt take the left hand I will go to the right, and if thou wilt go to the right hand then I will go to the left.

So Lot looked round and saw that the plain of Jor-dan was rich in grass, and would be a fine place for him and his herds to dwell in; so he made his choice at once, and went to live there.

Two large towns were on this plain, Sod-om and Go-mor-rah. The men in Sod-om were full of sin, yet Lot, though a good man, went to live there that he might have a chance to add to his wealth.

As soon as Lot had gone, the Lord told A-bra-ham that he would give to him and his heirs all that land as far as he could see it. And the tribe of A-bra-ham would be so great that no one could count them.

Now Sa-rah A-bra-ham's wife, had a hand-maid—that is, a maid-of-all-work—whose name was Ha-gar; and she came from E-gypt. Ha-gar did Sa-rah a great wrong, and Sa-rah drove her from the house, and she fled to the woods.

An an-gel of the Lord found Ha-gar there by a spring of wa-ter, and said to her, From whence didst thou come? and where wilt thou go? And she said she had fled from Sa-rah, whose maid she was.

And the an-gel said she must go back to Sa-rah and do as she wished her to do. And he told Ha-gar she would have a son whose name would be Ish-ma-el, and that he would live out of doors and be at strife with all men. So Ha-gar went back to Sa-rah, and in due time God gave her a son, who was called Ish-ma-el.

When A-bra-ham was an old man, God told him that he and Sa-rah should have a son, who should be called I-saac.

One day at the hour of noon, when A-bra-ham sat by the door of his tent, he looked up and saw three men quite near him. Then he ran out to meet them, and bowed his face to the ground. And A-bra-ham bade them sit down and rest, and let some wa-ter be brought that they might wash their feet.

No one in those days wore such shoes as are worn now. Some went bare-foot, and some wore just a sole tied to the foot with strings, which did not keep off the dust and dirt as our shoes do.

So when one came in from a long walk the first thing he did was to bathe his feet, as that gave rest and ease, and when guests came the bowl was brought for their use.

And A-bra-ham brought them food to eat, and stood by to wait on them; and when they had had their fill, went with them to show them the way.

In those days the Lord came down on the earth and spoke with men, and it is thought that one of these three was the Lord, and the two with him were an-gels.

**THE AN-GELS' VIS-IT.**

And the Lord told A-bra-ham that he meant to burn Sod-om and Go-mor-rah for the sins of those who dwelt there. This made A-bra-ham sad, and he said there might be a few good men there, and he begged the Lord to spare the towns for their sakes.

The Lord said he would do so if ten good men could be found there.

And the Lord left A-bra-ham and he went back to his tent. At the close of the day, Lot sat in the gate of Sod-om and two an-gels came there. And as soon as Lot saw them he rose up to meet them and bowed down with his face to the ground.

Then these an-gels told Lot to take out of Sod-om all those who were dear to him, and flee in great haste, as the Lord meant to set the place on fire.

They were told not to look back, but while on their way Lot's wife turned her head, which was a sign that her heart was in Sod-om, and she died where she stood, and turned to salt.

But Lot and his two girls reached Zo-ar at dawn of the next day. Then the Lord rained fire on Sod-om and Go-mor-rah, and they were burnt up in fierce flame, with all that lived there, and all that grew out of the ground.

In due time God gave A-bra-ham the son he had said he should have.

And the child grew, and as soon as it could eat, A-bra-ham made a great feast. And at this feast Sa-rah saw that Ha-gar's son, Ish-ma-el, made fun of her boy, and she begged A-bra-ham to cast him out. A-bra-ham did not wish to do this, but God spoke to him and told him to do as Sa-rah had said, for I-saac was to be the true heir. So the next day A-bra-ham gave food and drink to Ha-gar and sent her and her child out of his house.

And Ha-gar took her boy and went to the waste lands of Beer-she-ba.

And when there was nought for the child to drink, he grew weak, and was like to die. And Ha-gar laid him 'neath a bush and went off and sat down and hid her face, and wept, for she loved her boy ve-ry much and did not want to see him die.

## DE-STRUC-TION OF THE CIT-IES OF THE PLAIN.

And a voice spoke to Ha-gar out of the sky, and said, What ails thee, Ha-gar? Fear not, for God hath heard the voice of the lad where he is. Rise, lift up the lad and hold him in thine arms.

And the voice told her that her son should be the head of a great tribe. And as she raised her eyes she saw a well of wa-ter, and she ran to it and gave her son a drink and he was soon strong and well once more.

And God was kind to Ish-ma-el, and he grew, and made his home in the woods, and came to have great skill with the bow.

Now it was God's wish to try the faith of A-bra-ham to him.

And he told him to take his son, I-saac, and go to the land of Mo-ri-ah, and lay him on the al-tar he was to build on one of the mounts there. It was not a hard task to kill a lamb, and to burn it so that the smoke of it should rise up to God, like praise from the hearts of men. But how could A-bra-ham take his own dear son, I-saac, and lay him on the wood, and let him be burnt up like a lamb?

Yet God told him to do it, and A-bra-ham knew that it was safe for him to do as God said.

So he rose the next day and took two of his young men with him, and I-saac his son, and cut the wood the right length, and set out for the mount of which God had told him.

**HA-GAR AND ISH-MA-EL.**

And as they drew near the place he took the wood from the ass and laid it on I-saac's back, and took the fire in his hand and a knife, and the two went up the mount.

Now I-saac did not know what the Lord had told A-bra-ham to do, nor why his fa-ther took him up to the mount. And he said, Here is the fire and the wood, but where is the lamb?

And A-bra-ham said, My son, God will give us the lamb we need.

And when they came to the place, A-bra-ham piled up the stones and put the wood on them, and bound I-saac and laid him on the wood.

Then he drew forth the knife to kill his son. And just then a voice from the sky cried out, A-bra-ham! A-bra-ham! And A-bra-ham said, Here am I.

And the Lord told him to do no harm to I-saac, for now he knew that A-bra-ham loved him, since he would not spare his own dear son if it was God's wish that he should give him up.

And as A-bra-ham turned his head he saw a ram that was caught in a bush, and he took the ram and laid it on the wood, and burnt it in-stead of his son.

At the end of a few years A-bra-ham went to live at Heb-ron. And Sa-rah died there.

When I-saac grew up to be a man, A-bra-ham did not wish him to take a wife from the land of Ca-naan where they served strange gods.

So he sent one of his men to the land where he used to live to bring back a wife for I-saac.

And as he drew near to a large town in that land he made his cam-els kneel down by a well. And it was the time of day when the wo-men of the place went out to draw wa-ter from the well.

And the man whom A-bra-ham had sent, asked God to help him, and to let him know which one of them was to be I-saac's wife. And he said he would ask one of them for a drink, and if she was kind and gave him a drink, and let his cam-els quench their thirst, then he should know that she was the one God chose to be the wife of A-bra-ham's son.

**RE-BEK-AH AT THE WELL.**

And he raised his heart to God and said, O Lord God of A-bra-ham, give me good speed this day.

And while he yet spoke a fair young maid named Re-bek-ah went down to the well and came up with the jar she had filled. And the man ran to meet her, and said to her, Let me drink, I pray thee.

And she said, Drink, my Lord, and held the jar in her hand so that he could drink with ease.

Then she said, I will give thy cam-els a drink; and she went down to the well and drew for all the cam-els. And the man stood still, and was yet in doubt if this was the maid whom God chose to be I-saac's wife.

And as soon as the cam-els had drunk their fill, the man took a gold ear-ring, and two bands of gold for the wrists, and gave them to Re-bek-ah. And he said, Whose child art thou? tell me, I pray thee. And is there room in thy sire's house for us to lodge in?

The maid said that her sire's name was Beth-u-el, and that there was no lack of straw and food, and there was room in the house where he and his men might lodge.

The man was glad when he heard this, for he knew the Lord had led him, and had brought him to the house to which he was sent. And he bowed his head and gave thanks.

**RE-BEK-AH JOUR-NEY-ING TO I-SAAC.**

The next day Re-bek-ah and her maids went with A-bra-ham's head man. And they came to the land of Ca-naan.

At the close of the day I-saac went to walk in the fields, and as he raised his eyes he saw the cam-els on their way home, and he went out to meet them.

Re-bek-ah said to the man with whom she rode, What man is this that comes through the field to meet us?

And the man told her that it was A-bra-ham's son, I-saac.

Then the maid drew her veil round her so as to hide her face, and came down from the cam-el. And I-saac took her to his house and made her his wife. And A-bra-ham gave, all that he had to I-saac; and when he died he was laid by the side of Sa-rah, his wife, in the tomb he had bought at Mach-pe-lah.

**THE MEET-ING OF I-SAAC AND RE-BEK-AH.**

And to this day no one has had such faith or trust in God as did A-bra-ham.

# CHAPTER IV.

## JACOB AND ESAU.

I-SAAC and Re-bek-ah had two sons. Their names were Ja-cob and E-sau. E-sau was the first-born, and in those days the first-born son had what was called the birth-right. This made him chief of all the rest, and heir to the most of his sire's wealth.

When the boys grew up to be men, E-sau took to the fields and to out-door sports, while Ja-cob was a plain man and dwelt in tents. And I-saac was fond of E-sau, who killed the deer, and brought him the meat to eat. But Re-bek-ah was more fond of Ja-cob.

One day Ja-cob had made some food called pot-tage, and E-sau came in from the field and said, Feed me, I pray thee, with that pot-tage, for I am faint.

And Ja-cob said, Sell me thy birth-right.

And E-sau said, I am at the point of death, so what good will a birth-right do me?

So he sold his birth-right to Ja-cob—which was a wrong thing for him to do—and took the bread and meat, and ate and drank, and then went on his way.

Now there came a time when I-saac was an old man, and his eyes were dim, for he had not long to live. And he called E-sau to his bed-side and told him to go out with his bow and shoot a deer and bring him some of the meat he was so fond of, that he might eat it and bless E-sau ere he died.

And Re-bek-ah heard what I-saac had said to E-sau, and she told it to Ja-cob. And she said to him, Go now to the flock, and fetch me from thence two good kids, and I will make such a dish as thy fa-ther loves. And thou shalt bring it to him that he may eat, and that he may bless thee ere his death.

So Ja-cob did as he was told, and brought the kids to his mo-ther that she might cook them in a way that would please the good man of the house.

Then Re-bek-ah put some of E-sau's clothes on Ja-cob, and put the skins of goats on his hands, for E-sau's hands had on them a thick coat of hair. And then Ja-cob took the meat and the bread and went in to his fa-ther.

And I-saac said, Who art thou, my son?

**I-SAAC SPEAK-ING TO E-SAU.**

And Ja-cob said, I am E-sau, thy first-born. Rise, I pray thee, and eat of the deer's meat I have brought, that thy soul may bless me.

And I-saac said to Ja-cob, How is it that thou hast found it so soon, my son?

And he said, The Lord thy God brought it to me.

And I-saac said to Ja-cob, Come near, I pray thee, that I may feel thee, my son, and know if thou be my son E-sau or not. And Ja-cob went near to his fa-ther and he felt him, and said, The voice is Ja-cob's voice, but the hands are the hands of E-sau.

And he said, Art thou in truth my son E-sau?

And Ja-cob said, I am.

And he said, Bring near the food, and I will eat, that my soul may bless thee.

And Ja-cob brought it near to him, and he did eat, and he brought him wine and he drank.

And his fa-ther said to him, Come near now, and kiss me, my son.

And he came near, and gave him the kiss. Then the old man asked God to bless this whom he thought was his first-born, and make him great, and give him all good things.

Ja-cob was scarce yet gone out from his fa-ther when E-sau came in from the hunt. And he brought in a nice dish of meat, and said, Let my fa-ther rise and eat of the flesh of the deer, that thy soul may bless me.

And I-saac said, Who art thou?

And he said, I am thy son, thy first-born, E-sau.

And I-saac shook like a leaf, and said, Who? Where is he that took deer's meat and brought it to me so that I did eat ere this, and bless him? Yea, and he shall be blest.

When E-sau heard these words he cried out with great grief, and said to his fa-ther, Bless me too, O my fa-ther!

But I-saac said that he could not take from Ja-cob what was now his—though he had won it through fraud.

And E-sau said in his heart, My fa-ther will soon be dead, and then I will kill Ja-cob.

**JA-COB'S DREAM.**

And these words were told to Re-bek-ah, and she sent for Ja-cob and said to him that E-sau meant to kill him, and he must leave home at once and go and stay with her bro-ther La-ban till E-sau's wrath had cooled.

And Ja-cob went out from Beer-she-ba.

And as he went on his way he came to a place where he thought he would lie down and rest. The sun was set, the day had been a long one, and he was quite worn out. So he put some stones for his head to rest on, and was soon sound a-sleep.

And while he slept he had a strange dream. He saw a flight of steps that stood on the ground, the top of which was far, far up in the sky. And bright an-gels went up and down the steps. And the Lord stood at the top, and said, I am with thee, and will take care of thee, and will bring thee back to this land, for I will not leave thee till I have done that which I have told thee of.

And Ja-cob woke out of his sleep, and said, 'Tis true the Lord is in this place, and I knew it not.

And he was in great fear, and said, This is the house of God, and this is the gate of heav-en!

Then he rose up and took the stone on which his head had lain and set it up on end, and he poured oil on top of it. And he gave to that place the name of Beth-el, and made a vow to love and serve God all the rest of his life.

And though he had done wrong, God for-gave him, and he was known as a great and good man.

# CHAPTER V.

## JACOB AND RACHEL.

AS Ja-cob went on his way to the East he came to a well that was out in the field, near which lay three great flocks of sheep. And there was a great stone on top of the well. And the men who took care of the flocks would roll the stone from the mouth of the well, and give drink to the sheep. Then they would roll the stone back to the mouth of the well.

Ja-cob said to the men, Whence do ye come?

And they told him.

And he said, Know ye La-ban, the son of Na-hor?

**RA-CHEL AND JA-COB AT THE WELL.**

And they said, We know him.

And he said, Is he well?

And they said, He is well. And there is one of his girls now, Ra-chel, and she comes this way with her sheep.

While Ja-cob yet spake with the men, Ra-chel came up with the sheep that she took care of. And when Ja-cob saw her, he came near, and drew the stone from the mouth of the well, and gave drink to the whole of her flock.

And as soon as he told her that he was Re-bek-ah's son, she ran home with the news.

And when La-ban heard that his sis-ter's son was near, he ran out to meet him, and threw his arms round his neck and kissed him, and brought him to his house.

And Ja-cob dwelt there for the space of a month.

And La-ban said to Ja-cob, Thou art bone of my bone and flesh of my flesh, but it is not right for thee to serve me for nought. Tell me how much I shall pay thee?

Now La-ban had two girls—Le-ah and Ra-chel. And Ja-cob was in love with Ra-chel; and he said to La-ban, I will serve thee se-ven years if thou wilt give me Ra-chel for a wife.

And La-ban said it would please him to have Ja-cob for a son-in-law, and Ja-cob served sev-en years for Ra-chel, and they seemed to him but a few days, so great was his love for her. And at the end of that time Ja-cob said to La-ban, Give me my wife, for I have served thee my full time.

And La-ban made a feast, and brought in Le-ah to be Ja-cob's wife. In those days the bride wore a veil, and the man she wed could not look on her face till the next day.

So Ja-cob did not find out this trick till the next morn, and then he came in great wrath to La-ban and said, What is this thou hast done to us? Did I not serve with thee for Ra-chel? and why did'st thou cheat me?

And La-ban said, In our land the first-born must wed the first. Serve me sev-en years more, and thou shalt have Ra-chel for a wife. And Ja-cob did so, and though he dwelt with both—which was thought to be no sin in those days—he was far more fond of Ra-chel than he was of Le-ah.

Le-ah bore Ja-cob a host of sons, but it was years ere Ra-chel had a child. And this made her sad. But at last she had a son, and she called his name Jo-seph. And as soon as Jo-seph was born Ja-cob told La-ban to give him his wives and all the goods that he owned, and let him go back to the land he came from.

But La-ban begged him to stay. He had found, he said, that the Lord had blest him for Ja-cob's sake, and he might have some of the land and the flocks if he would still serve him.

So Ja-cob took care of La-ban's flocks, and had sheep and goats of his own, and things went well for a time.

But one day Ja-cob heard La-ban's sons say some hard things of him, and he saw that La-ban did not give him the kind looks that he used to. And he felt that the time had come for them to part. And the Lord told Ja-cob to go back to the land he came from, and he would deal well with him. And Ja-cob took his wives, and the flocks and the goods he owned, and set out for the land of Ca-naan.

Ja-cob sent one of his men to E-sau to say that he was on his way home, and was in hopes he would find grace in his sight.

And the man brought back word that E-sau was on his way to meet Ja-cob with a large force of men. And Ja-cob thought of the wrongs he had done his broth-er, and was in great fear of him.

He sought the help of God, and God told him what to do. And Ja-cob sent great droves of sheep and goats, and ewes and rams, and ca-mels and colts, and cows, and choice ones from all his live stock, as a gift to E-sau.

And at night, when no one else was near, a man whose face shone with a strange light, came to Ja-cob and wound his arms round him and tried to throw him. And the two strove so hard that Ja-cob's thigh was put out of joint.

And as it grew light the man said, Let me go, for the day breaks.

Ja-cob said, I will not let thee go till thou hast blest me.

And the man said, What is thy name? And he said, Ja-cob.

And he said, Thy name shall be no more Ja-cob but Is-ra-el, for as a prince thou hast pow-er with God and with men.

And when he had blest Ja-cob he went his way. And Ja-cob gave the place the name of Pe-ni-el, for, said he, I have seen God face to face and my life has been spared. For Ja-cob knew by this that E-sau would not kill him.

**THE MEET-ING OF JA-COB AND E-SAU.**

When Ja-cob was an old, old man Ra-chel bore him a son; and they called his name Ben-ja-min. And Ra-chel died. And it was hard for Ja-cob to have her die and leave him, for his love for her was great, and she was a good wife to him.

# CHAPTER VI.

## JOSEPH AND HIS BRETHREN.

JA-COB had twelve sons, and he was more fond of Jo-seph than of all the rest; for he was the child of his old age. And he gave him a fine coat, and made a great pet of him. This did not please the rest of the sons, and they showed their hate of Jo-seph in all sorts of ways.

One night Jo-seph had a strange dream, and he told it to Le-vi, Sim-e-on, and the rest, and it made them hate him all the more.

He said, As we bound sheaves in the field, lo, my sheaf rose and stood up straight. And your sheaves stood round, and bowed to my sheaf.

And those who heard him said, Shalt thou in-deed reign o'er us? And his words and his deeds filled them with a fierce hate.

And it was not long ere he told them of a fresh dream he had had, in which he saw the sun and moon and e-lev-en stars bow down to him. And he told it to Ja-cob, and his e-lev-en sons.

And Ja-cob took him to task, and said to him, What does this dream mean? Are all of us to bow down to the earth to thee? And he made up his mind to watch these signs, which might be sent of God.

**JO-SEPH'S DREAM.**

Now Ja-cob had large flocks of sheep and goats at Shech-em, and all of his sons but Jo-seph had gone there to feed them. And Ja-cob said to Jo-seph, Go and see if it be well with thy breth-ren, and with the flocks, and bring me back word.

And Jo-seph went out from the vale of Heb-ron to the land of Shech-em.

When he came there he found that his broth-ers had gone on to Do-than. And Jo-seph went to Do-than and found them. And as soon as he came in sight they thought of a way in which they might get rid of him.

**SHECH-EM, THE FIRST CAP-I-TAL OF THE KING-DOM OF IS-RAEL.**

Come, let us kill him, they said; and throw him in-to a pit, and say that a wild beast ate him up. Then we shall see what will be-come of his dreams.

But Reu-ben heard it, and saved him out of their hands. And he said, Let us not kill the lad. Shed no blood; but cast him in-to this pit, and lay no hand on him. For he meant to take him out of the pit, and bear him home to his fath-er.

But when Jo-seph came near these men who should have been kind to him, they took off his coat and threw him in-to the pit, which was dry, or he would have drowned. These old dry wells were left as traps in which to catch the wild beasts that prowled round in the dead of night, and well these bad men knew what would be Jo-seph's fate.

As they sat down to eat, they looked up and saw a lot of men and cam-els on their way to E-gypt, with spices, and balm and myrrh.

**JO-SEPH SOLD BY HIS BROTH-ERS.**

And Ju-dah—one of Ja-cob's sons—said, Let us not kill the lad, for he is of our own flesh, but let us sell him to these men. And the rest thought it was a good scheme. So they drew Jo-seph up out of the pit and sold him for a small sum, and those who bought the lad took him down with them to E-gypt.

And the bad men took Jo-seph's coat and dipped it in the blood of a kid they had slain. And they brought it to Ja-cob, and said, This have we found. Is it thy son's coat?

And Ja-cob knew it at once, and said, It is my son's coat. Jo-seph has no doubt been the prey of some wild beast. And his grief was great.

The men who bought Jo-seph brought him down to E-gypt and sold him to Pot-i-phar for a slave.

And the Lord was with Jo-seph, who served Pot-i-phar so well, that the rich man put him in charge of his home and lands. But Pot-i-phar's wife told false tales, and Jo-seph, who had done no wrong, was thrust in-to jail. Pha-ra-oh was then king of E-gypt. And it came to pass that he fell out with his but-ler and chief cook, and had them shut up in the same place where Jo-seph was bound.

And the man on guard put them in charge of Jo-seph, who went in and out of the ward as he chose. And one morn when he came in to them he saw they were sad, and asked them why it was.

And they said, We have dreamed dreams, and there is no one to tell us what they mean.

And Jo-seph said, Tell me them, I pray you.

And the chief but-ler told his dream to Jo-seph first. And he said, In my dream I saw a vine, that put forth three branch-es and brought forth ripe grapes.

And Jo-seph said to him, In three days shall Pha-ra-oh lift up thine head, and put thee back in thy place, and thou shalt serve him as of old. But think of me when it shall be well with thee; speak of me to the king, and bring me out of this house.

And the but-ler said that he would.

**JO-SEPH'S COAT.**

Then the chief cook told his dream; and he said, In my dream I had three white bas-kets on my head. And in the top one were all sorts of bake meats for the king. And the birds did eat out of the bas-ket that I bore on my head.

And Jo-seph said to him, In three days shall Pha-ra-oh lift up thy head and hang thee on a tree; and the birds shall eat the flesh from thy bones.

The third day was the king's birth-day, and he made a great feast. And he put the chief but-ler back in his place, and hung the chief cook; just as Jo-seph had said he would do. But the chief but-ler gave not a thought to Jo-seph, nor spoke one good word for him to the king, as he had said he would.

Two years from this time the king had a dream, from which he woke, and then fell a-sleep and dreamt the self-same dream. This was such a strange thing that it made the king feel ill at ease. And he sent for all the wise men in the land to tell him what these dreams meant.

Then the chief but-ler spoke to the king, and said that when he and the cook were in jail, there was a young man there, a Jew, whom the chief of the guard made much use of. And we told him our dreams, and he told us what they meant. And it came out just as he said.

Then the king sent at once for Jo-seph, and said to him: In my dream I stood on the bank of the Nile. And there came up out of the riv-er sev-en fat cows, and they fed in a field near by. Then sev-en lean cows came up that were naught but skin and bone. And the lean cows ate up the fat cows. And yet no one would have known it, for they were just as lean as when I first saw them. Then I woke, but soon fell a-sleep once more.

Then I dreamt, and in my dream I saw sev-en ears of corn come up on one stalk, full and good. And lo, sev-en ears that were thin and dried up with the east wind sprang up af-ter them. And the poor ears ate up the good ones.

Jo-seph said, For sev-en years there will be no lack of food in the land, and all will go well; and then there will come a time of great want, and rich and poor will be in need of food, and not a few will starve to death. Let the king choose a wise man to see that corn is laid up in the land when the good years bring the rich growth, so that there will be no lack of food in the years when the crops are small.

**PHA-RA-OH'S DREAM.**

And the king said to Jo-seph, Since God hath showed thee all this there is none so wise as thou art. So he put him in charge of all the land of E-gypt, and he was to rank next to the king. And the king took a ring from his own hand and put it on Jo-seph's hand, and when he rode out, men bowed the knee, and his word was law in all the land. And Jo-seph took a wife, and he who was brought to E-gypt a slave, was now a rich man.

And there came years when the grain grew rank in the fields, and the crops were large. And Jo-seph saw that a large part of it was laid up, and that there was no waste of the good food. For the end of those rich years came and then there was a time of dearth in all the lands, when the earth would not yield, and men and beasts were in want of food.

But there was no lack of corn in E-gypt. And Jo-seph sold the corn that he had stored in the barns, and crowds came in to buy it.

When Ja-cob heard that corn could be bought in E-gypt, he told his sons to go down and buy some, that they might not starve to death.

And ten of them went down to buy corn in E-gypt. But Ja-cob kept Ben-ja-min at home, for fear he would be lost to him as Jo-seph was lost.

## JO-SEPH AND HIS BROTH-ERS.

When Ja-cob's ten sons came to the place where Jo-seph was, they bowed down to the ground. And Jo-seph knew them at once, but they did not know him, or give a thought to his dreams.

And Jo-seph spoke in a rough voice, and said, Whence come ye?

And they said, From the land of Ca-naan to buy food.

And he said, Ye are spies, and have come to see how poor the land is.

And they said to him, Nay, my lord, but to buy food are we come. We are all one man's sons; and we are true men, and not spies.

But Jo-seph would have it that they were spies.

And they said, There were twelve of us, sons of one man. Young Ben-ja-min is at home with his fa-ther, and one is dead.

And Jo-seph said, Go prove that ye are not spies; let one of the ten that are here go and fetch the young lad, Ben-ja-min. And he put them in jail for three days. And he said, Let one of you be bound, and kept in the guard-house, while the rest of you take back the corn that you need. And they said that they would do this.

Then he took Sim-e-on from their midst, and had him bound, and put in the guard-house.

And he sent word to his men to fill their sacks with corn, and to put back the price in each sack, and to give them food to eat on the way. And thus did Jo-seph do good to those who did ill to him.

When Ja-cob's nine sons went home they told all that had been said and done to them, and that the lord of the land bade them bring Ben-ja-min down to E-gypt or he would think they were spies, and their lives would not be safe.

Ja-cob said, My son shall not go down with you, for his broth-er is dead, and he is all I have left. If harm should come to him on the way, I should die of grief.

**THE MEET-ING OF JO-SEPH AND BEN-JA-MIN.**

When the corn they had brought from E-gypt was all gone, Ja-cob told his sons to go down and buy more. And Ju-dah spoke up and said, The man swore we should not see his face if Ben-ja-min was not with us. If thou wilt send him with us we will go; but if thou wilt not send him we will not go down.

Then Ja-cob said, If it must be so, take Ben-ja-min with you, and may God give you grace with this man that he may send my two boys back to me.

So the men took Ben-ja-min and went down to E-gypt, and stood face to face with Jo-seph.

And they gave Jo-seph the gifts they had brought, and bowed down to the earth. And he asked how they all were, and if their fath-er was well; and when he saw Ben-ja-min he said, Is this the young broth-er of whom you spoke? And he said to the lad, God be good to thee, my son.

And Jo-seph's heart was so full at sight of the boy, and he longed so to throw his arms round him, that he had to make haste and leave the room that his tears might not be seen.

Then he came back and had the feast set out, and all did eat and drink, and were glad at heart. And when the time came for his guests to leave, Jo-seph told his head man to fill their sacks with corn, to put their gold back in the mouth of the sacks, and to put in the young lad's sack the cup from which Jo-seph drank at each meal.

This was done, and when they had gone out of the town Jo-seph bade his man go and say to them: My lord's cup is lost, and you must know who stole it.

And when the man came up with Ja-cob's sons, he said just what Jo-seph told him to say. And they were all in a rage, and said: Why does my lord say such things of us? If the cup is found on one of us, kill him; and make the rest of us slaves.

And each one of them cast his sack on the ground, and loosed it at the top. And the cup was found in Ben-ja-min's sack. Then they rent their clothes, and in great grief went back to Jo-seph's house and found him there. And they fell down at his feet.

**JA-COB BLESS-ES JO-SEPH'S CHIL-DREN.**

And Ju-dah said, God has found out our sins. Let us be your slaves; and take him as well in whose sack the cup was found.

Jo-seph said, No; but the man in whose sack the cup was found shall stay and serve me, and the rest shall go in peace.

Then Ju-dah, who had sworn that he would bring back the boy, said to Jo-seph: If we go home, and our fath-er sees the lad is not with us, he will die of grief. For his life is bound up in the lad's life.

Jo-seph could not keep back his tears, and when he had sent all the men of E-gypt out of the room, he said to his broth-ers, Come near, I pray you.

And they came near. And he said, I am Jo-seph, whom ye sold in-to E-gypt. But grieve not that ye did this thing, for God did send me here that I might save your lives. Go home and tell my fath-er that God hath made me lord of all E-gypt, and bid him come down to me at once. And say that he shall dwell near me, in the land of Go-shen, and I will take care of him.

Then he fell on Ben-ja-min's neck, and they wept; and he kissed his broth-ers and shed tears, but they were tears of joy.

Ja-cob took all that he had and went down to E-gypt. And three-score and ten souls went with him. And they dwelt in the land of Go-shen, and Ja-cob died there.

Jo-seph's breth-ren thought that he would hate them now that their fath-er was dead. And they fell down at his feet and wept and prayed that he would do them no harm.

Jo-seph bade them fear not, for he would take care of them and be kind to them. They had meant to do him an ill turn when he was a lad, but God had made it turn out for good, and it was all right. And Jo-seph lived to a good old age, and had two sons, whose names were E-phra-im and Ma-nas-seh.

# CHAPTER VII.

## THROUGH THE RED SEA AND THE WILDERNESS.

BY and by there rose up a new King in E-gypt who knew not Jo-seph. He was called Pha-ra-oh, as this was the name by which all the kings of E-gypt were known. And he said there were more He-brews, or Jews, in the land than there ought to be, and if war should break out, and these Jews should take sides with the foes of Pha-ra-oh and his race, they would be sure to win. So he set them hard tasks, and made them bear great loads, and did all he could to vex them, and still they grew in strength. God had said they were to be as the stars in the sky, and as the sands of the sea, that no one could count. And the king of E-gypt tried to stop this thing.

And he made it a law that if a boy child was born to the He-brews it should be put to death at once; but a girl child might live. And this was the cause of great grief to the poor bond-slaves, who were forced to do the will of the great king.

One day the prin-cess went down to bathe in the stream that ran near her house. And her maids went with her. And as she stood on the shore of the Nile, she caught sight of a small boat built like an ark, that was hid in the reeds, and sent her maids to fetch it out.

When the prin-cess looked in the ark she saw the child. And the babe wept. And the prin-cess tried to soothe it, but the child cried the more, for her voice was a strange one. And she said, This is a He-brew child.

And one of her maids spoke up, and said, Shall I get thee a He-brew nurse, that she may nurse the child for thee?

And the prin-cess said, Yes; go.

And the maid brought her own and the babe's moth-er, to whom the prin-cess said, Take this child and nurse it for me, and I will pay thee for it.

And the wo-man took the child and took care of it.

**THE FIND-ING OF MO-SES.**

And the child grew, and was brought down to Pha-ra-oh's house, and the prin-cess made him her son, and gave him the name of Mo-ses: which means "Drawn out."

One day, when Mo-ses had grown to be a man, he went out to look at those of his own race, and to watch them at their tasks. And while he stood there a man from E-gypt struck one of the Jews; and when Mo-ses looked to the right and to the left and saw that no one was near, he slew the one from E-gypt and hid him in the sand.

And the next day, when he went out, he saw there was a fight be-tween two He-brews. And he said to the one who was in the wrong, Why did you strike that man?

And he said, Who made thee our judge? Dost thou want to kill me, as thou didst the one from E-gypt?

And Mo-ses was scared, for he thought no one knew of this deed.

As soon as it came to the ears of the king, he sought to slay Mo-ses. But Mo-ses fled from him, and dwelt in the land of Mid-i-an, and found a wife there, and took care of the flocks of Jeth-ro, his wife's fath-er.

One day as he led his flock out in search of food he came to Mount Ho-reb, and there he saw a flame of fire stream out of a bush, and the bush was not burnt in the least.

As he drew near the bush the Lord spoke to him out of the flame, and Mo-ses hid his face, for he dared not look on God.

The Lord said, The cry of the chil-dren of Is-ra-el has come up to me, and I have seen how ill they have been used. And I will send thee to Pha-ra-oh that thou mayst bring them forth out of the land of E-gypt.

But Mo-ses was loth to go.

**MO-SES BROUGHT BE-FORE PHA-RA-OH'S DAUGH-TER.**

And the Lord said, What is that in thine hand? And Mo-ses said, A rod, And the Lord said, Cast it on the ground. And he cast it on the ground, and it was changed to a snake, and Mo-ses fled from it. Then the Lord said to Mo-ses, Put forth thine hand, and take it by the tail. And Mo-ses did so, and it was a rod in his hand. And the Lord said, Put now thy hand in on thy breast. And he put it in, and when he drew it out it was white, and like a dead hand. And he put his hand in once more, and drew it out, and it was like the rest of his flesh.

Then Mo-ses said, O, my Lord, I am not fit to do this work, for I am slow of speech, and a man of few words.

And the Lord said to him, I will be with thee, and teach thee what thou wilt say.

Still Mo-ses was loth to go, and the Lord was wroth with him, and said, Take Aa-ron with thee. He can speak well. And thou shalt tell him what to say and do, and I will teach you, and with this rod in thy hand thou shalt do great things, as if thou wert God.

So Mo-ses took his wife and his sons and put them on an ass, and went back to E-gypt with the rod of God in his hand.

And Mo-ses and Aa-ron went in to the king and begged him to let the He-brews go out of the land. And he would not, but laid more work on the men, and bade them make bricks with-out straw, and do all sorts of hard tasks.

And the Lord sent plagues on the land, and the ponds dried up, and all the large streams were turned to blood, and the fish died, and the stench of them made the air scarce fit to breathe. And there was no wa-ter they could drink. Then there came a plague of frogs, and they were so thick in the land that Pha-ra-oh said he would let the chil-dren of Is-ra-el go if Mo-ses would rid him of the frogs at the same time.

But the king did not keep his word, for as soon as he found the frogs grew less, he said the He-brews should not go.

Then the Lord smote the land with lice; but still Pha-ra-oh's heart was hard.

**MOS-ES AT THE BURN-ING BUSH.**

Then the Lord sent flies in such swarms that there was no place that was free from them, and they made the food not fit to eat.

And the king told Mo-ses he would let the bond-slaves go to serve their God, but they were not to go far till the land was rid of flies. Then Mo-ses went forth and prayed to God, and the flies left the land. But still the king's heart was hard, and he would not let them go.

Then the Lord sent worse plagues: the flocks and herds died; there were boils on man and beast; the crops did not come up, and rain, hail, and balls of fire came down from the sky. And still the heart of the king was as hard as stone. Then the Lord sent lo-custs, that ate up all the hail had left, and there was not a green leaf on the trees nor a blade of grass to be seen in the whole land.

And the king bade Mo-ses to set him free from this plague. And the Lord sent a strong west wind, that blew the flies in-to the Red Sea. Yet Pha-ra-oh would not let the He-brews go.

Then the Lord told Mo-ses to stretch out his hand, and there came up a thick cloud that made the land so dark that the folks staid in bed for three days. And Pha-ra-oh said to Mo-ses, Get thee out of my sight. For if I see thy face thou shalt die.

And Mo-ses said, Thou hast well said: I will see thy face no more.

And the Lord sent one more plague on E-gypt: he smote the first-born of men and of beasts, and a great cry was heard through the land. And then Pha-ra-oh had to let the chil-dren of Is-ra-el go, for he could not keep up this strife with God. And Mo-ses led the He-brew chil-dren out of E-gypt, and the Lord sent a cloud by day and a fire by night to show them the way.

And when they were in camp by the Red Sea, they looked up and saw Pha-ra-oh and his hosts, and were in great fear lest he should kill them. And they cried out to the Lord, and blamed Mo-ses that he had brought them in-to such straits.

**MIR-I-AM, THE SIS-TER OF MO-SES, AND THE WO-MEN OF IS-RAEL SING-ING PRAISES.**

As they came to the Red Sea, Mo-ses raised his rod and the sea rose like a wall on each side, and the chil-dren of Is-ra-el went on dry land through the midst of the sea.

Then Pha-ra-oh and his hosts came close in the rear, and passed down be-tween the great sea-wall that rose at the right hand and at the left. And the waves that had stood still at a sign from God were let loose, and the king and his horse-men were swept out of sight.

When the chil-dren of Is-ra-el came out of the Red Sea they were three days with naught to drink. And when they came to a stream, called Ma-rah, they found it bitter. And they said to Mo-ses, What shall we drink?

And Mo-ses cried out to the Lord, and the Lord showed him a tree, and when he had cast a branch of it in the stream it was made sweet at once. And they came to E-lim, where were ten wells and three-score palm-trees, and there they made their camp.

It was not long ere there was a great cry for bread.

And Mo-ses plead with God, and when the sun went down that day quails flew in-to the camp, and they had all the meat they cared to eat. At dawn of the next day, as soon as the dew was off the ground, there came a rain of what was at first thought to be hail-stones.

**THE CROSS-ING OF THE RED SEA.**

But Mo-ses said it was food that God had sent them to eat, and they were to take all and no more than they would need for one day. For they were to trust in God that he would feed them each day. On the sixth day they were to take what would last them for two days, for no food fell on the day of rest.

This new food was called man-na.

As they went on they came to Reph-i-dim, but found no wa-ter to drink. And they found fault with Mo-ses. And Mo-ses cried out, Lord, what shall I do to these, who have a mind to stone me?

At this time they were near Mount Ho-reb, where God spoke to Mo-ses out of a bush that was on fire, yet not burnt.

**MO-SES AND THE TA-BLES OF THE LAW.**

And God told Mo-ses to take his rod in his hand and go on till he came to a rock. And this rock he was to strike with his rod, and wa-ter would flow out of it. And Mo-ses did as the Lord told him, and when he struck the rock the wa-ter ran out.

In the third month from the time they left E-gypt, the chil-dren of Is-ra-el came near Mount Si-na-i, and went in-to camp. And Mo-ses went up to the top of the Mount, and the Lord spoke to him there.

On the third day a thick cloud of smoke rose from Mount Si-na-i, and a loud noise that made those that heard it quake with fear. And Mo-ses led his flock out of the camp, and they came and stood at the foot of the mount. And they said to Mo-ses, Speak thou with us, and we will hear; but let not God speak with us lest we die. But Mo-ses told them that God had not come to make them die, but to make them fear to do aught that did not please him.

And God gave to Mo-ses two blocks of stone on which were the Ten Laws that the chil-dren of Is-ra-el were to keep.

**WELL AND PALM-TREES IN THE DES-ERT.**

**THE RIV-ER NILE IN E-GYPT.**

Now while Mo-ses was in the mount, face to face with God, those whom he had brought out of E-gypt were in camp at the foot. And Mo-ses staid so long that they made up their minds he would not come back. So they said to Aa-ron, Make us a God that we can bow down to. And Aa-ron bade them throw all the gold they had in-to the fire. And they did so, and it took the form of a calf. And when God saw this he was not pleased, but bade Mo-ses make haste down the mount.

When Mo-ses came down from the mount with the two flat stones in his hands, and drew near the camp, and saw what had been done, he was in a great rage. He cast the blocks of stone out of his hands and broke them at the foot of the mount.

Then he took the calf which they had made, and burnt it in the fire till there was nought left of it but a fine dust. And Mo-ses begged God to blot out the sins of those whom he had led out of E-gypt.

And the Lord told Mo-ses to hew out two blocks of stone like to the first, and bring them up with him to the top of Mount Si-na-i.

This Mo-ses did, and the Lord wrote on them the Ten Laws that all were to keep if they would reach the land they sought.

They were more than two-score years on the road, and in that time they met with plagues, and there was strife in their midst, yet as they went there was the fire by night and the cloud by day to show that the Lord was with them.

When they came to Mount Hor and were yet a long way from Ca-naan, Aa-ron died, and there was great grief at his loss. They were sick at heart and foot-sore, and spoke hard words of God and Mo-ses. There is no bread here for us, they said, and no wa-ter, and we loathe this man-na. And for this sin God sent snakes in-to their camp, and they bit the chil-dren of Is-ra-el so that a few of them died. Then they plead with Mo-ses to rid them of the snakes, and make their peace with God.

And Mo-ses prayed for them. And God told him to make a snake like to those which bit his flock, and set it up on a pole. And all those who would look at this brass snake should be made well.

**MOS-ES ON MOUNT SINAI.**

And Mo-ses did so. And this sign was meant to show forth Christ, who was to heal men of their sins, and to be raised up on a cross.

## BA-LAAM AND THE ASS.

And Mo-ses led his flock till they came to the plains of Mo-ab. And Ba-lak, the king of that land, thought they had come to fight with him, and he sent a man named Ba-laam out to curse them and drive them back. He told Ba-laam he would make him a rich man if he would do this thing, and as Ba-laam was fond of wealth he said he would do the king's will. So he set forth on his ass, and had not gone far when he met an an-gel with a drawn sword in his hand. Ba-laam did not see him, but the ass did and turned out of the road. But the an-gel went on and stood in a place where there was a wall on each side.

When the ass came to the place she went close to the wall and tried to get by. But she hurt Ba-laam's foot and he struck her and made her go on. And the an-gel went on and stood in a place where there was no room to turn to the right hand or the left.

Then the ass shook with fright and fell down on the ground. And Ba-laam struck her with the staff that he had in his hand.

And the Lord made the ass speak like a man, and say, What have I done to thee that thou hast struck me these three times?

Ba-laam said, To make thee move on: I would there were a sword in my hand, for I would kill thee.

Then the ass said, Am I not thine? and have I been wont to do so to thee? And Ba-laam said, No. Then the Lord made Ba-laam see the an-gel that stood in the way with a drawn sword in his hand, and Ba-laam bowed his face to the ground.

Then the an-gel said, Why hast thou struck thine ass these three times? Lo, I came out to stop thee, and to turn thee from the way of sin. And the ass saw me, and turned from the path, and if she had not done so I would have slain thee.

Then he said to Ba-laam, Go with the men the king has sent, but say on-ly what I shall tell thee.

So Ba-laam went with the men, and when Ba-lak heard that he was come he went out to meet him. The next day Ba-lak took Ba-laam to a high place, from whence he could look down on the camp of Is-ra-el, and curse them.

But the Lord would not let him curse them, but made him speak good things of them. This was done on three high mounts, and at last the king was wroth, and said to Ba-laam, I sent for thee to curse my foes, and lo, these three times hast thou blest them.

**MO-SES ON MOUNT NE-BO.**

And Ba-lak bade him make haste and go back to his own home. And Ba-laam went off as poor as he came, for Ba-lak gave him none of his gold.

The Lord brought Mo-ses and his flock to the banks of the Jor-dan, which they would have to cross to reach the land of Ca-naan. And while they were there, Mo-ses went up to the top of Mount Ne-bo to talk with God. And God told him how large the land was that he would give to the chil-dren of Is-ra-el. And he said that Mo-ses should look on it, but should not step foot in the land. And Mo-ses died on Mount Ne-bo, and though an old man, was well and strong till the Lord took him. And no one knows in what part of the earth his grave was made.

# CHAPTER VIII.

## HOW JOSHUA AND JEPHTHAH FOUGHT FOR THE LORD.

WHEN Mo-ses died, Josh-u-a took charge of the chil-dren of Is-ra-el, and sought to do God's will, as Mo-ses had done. And Josh-u-a sent word through the camp that in three days they would cross the Jor-dan. And when they set foot in the stream the waves stood back as they did in the Red Sea, and they went through Jor-dan on dry ground. And as they came up out of the stream the waves closed up and there was no path-way through them.

The chil-dren of Is-ra-el made their camp at a place called Gil-gal; and as there was no lack of food in this good land, the Lord ceased to rain down man-na for them to eat.

The next day Josh-u-a left the camp and came near to the walls of Jer-i-cho. There he met a man with a drawn sword in his hand. And Josh-u-a said, Art thou for us or for our foes?

And the man said, As prince of the Lord's host am I now come. And at these words Josh-u-a fell on his face to the earth; for he knew it was the Lord that spoke to him.

**PASS-ING THROUGH THE JOR-DAN.**

The Lord told Josh-u-a to have no fear of the king of Jer-i-cho, for the children of Is-ra-el should take the town. All their men of war were to march round the town once each day for six days. Some of the priests were to bear the ark, which held the things they made use of when they went in to talk with God, and some were to blow on rams' horns.

And the next day—when the six days were at an end—they were to march round the town sev-en times, and the priests were to blow their horns. And when the men of Is-ra-el heard a long loud blast they were all to give a great shout and the wall would fall flat to the ground, and they could march in and take the town.

Josh-u-a bade his men do all the Lord had said; and told them to make no noise with their voice as they went their rounds till he bade them shout. And when the priests blew their horns for the last time, Josh-u-a cried, Shout! for the Lord is with us! and there was a great shout and the wall fell, and they took the town; and the fame of Josh-u-a spread through all the lands.

Josh-u-a fought with more than a score of kings and won their lands from them; but yet there was much land in Ca-naan for which the chil-dren of Is-ra-el would have to fight.

But as the years went on, Josh-u-a grew so old that he could not lead his men to war as he used to do. And he called his flock to him and told them how good the Lord had been to them. And he bade them love the Lord and serve him, and put from them all strange gods. He said, Choose ye this day whom ye will serve; but as for me and my house we will serve the Lord.

**JOSH-U-A AND THE STONE OF WIT-NESS.**

And the men said, The Lord hath done great things for us, and him will we serve, for he is our God.

And Josh-u-a took a great stone and set it up 'neath an oak tree that stood near where the ark was kept at Shi-loh. And this stone, he said, was to be a sign of the vow they had made there to serve the Lord. And when the talk was at an end, the men went to their own homes.

And ere long Josh-u-a died. And they laid him in the part of the land that God gave him as his own, on the north side of the hill of Ga-ash.

Then the chil-dren of Is-ra-el went to war with the tribes that were in the land of Ca-naan, as Josh-u-a had told them to do. But they did not drive them all out, as they should have done, but made friends with those that were left, and were led in-to sin, and were made to serve as bond-slaves. And when they were sick of their sins, and sought the help of the Lord, he sent men to rule them, and to lead them out to war and set them free from these friends who proved to be the worst kind of foes.

Now there was a man in Is-ra-el whose name was Jeph-thah. He was a brave man, and had done great deeds, but the chil-dren of Is-ra-el were not kind to him, so he fled from their land, and went to live in the land of Tob. But when the Jews had need of a man to lead them out to war, they thought of Jeph-thah. And they said, Come, and be at the head of us when we go out to fight the Am-mon-ites.

And Jeph-thah said, If I go with you, and win the fight, will you make me judge in Is-ra-el?

And they said they would.

Now ere the fight took place, Jeph-thah made a vow that if the Lord would let him win he would give to God—that is, would slay and burn as if it were a lamb—the first who came out of his doors to meet him when he went back to his home.

Jeph-thah should not have made this rash vow, and need not have kept it if he had asked God to for-give the sin.

He went out to fight the Am-mon-ites, and by the help of the Lord the chil-dren of Is-ra-el were set free from them.

**JEPH-THAH AND HIS DAUGH-TER.**

When the fight was at an end Jeph-thah went back to his home, and the first to come out to meet him was his own child, a fair young maid, whose face was bright with joy. She was all the child that Jeph-thah had, and when he saw her he rent his clothes and told her of the vow he had made.

And she said, My fath-er, if thou hast made a vow to the Lord, do with me as thou hast said. And he took his child and did to her as he had said he would, and all the young girls in Is-ra-el wept for her.

Jeph-thah was a judge for six years, and then he died.

# CHAPTER IX.

## SAMSON: THE STRONG MAN.

THE Jews kept on in their sins, and took no pains to please the Lord, and so fell in-to the hands of the Phil-is-tines.

And there was at that time a man in Is-ra-el whose name was Ma-no-ah. Both he and his wife served the Lord; and they had no child. And God sent one of his an-gels to the wife of Ma-no-ah to tell her that she should have a son who was to be brought up to serve the Lord, and to do his work.

Ere long Ma-no-ah and his wife had a son, to whom they gave the name of Sam-son.

And the child grew, and the Lord blest him. And when he was grown up he went to Tin-muth, where he met a Phil-is-tine wo-man and fell in love with her.

Then his pa-rents plead with him to find a wife in Is-ra-el, and not to take this one who was no friend to his race. But Sam-son would not give her up.

So they went with him to Tin-muth. And on the way a li-on ran out and roared at him. And Sam-son put his arms round the beast and tore him with his hands as if he had been a young kid. But he did not tell his fath-er and moth-er what he had done.

The time soon came when Sam-son was to set the Jews free from the Phil-is-tines. And he went down to one of their towns and slew a few of their men, and then went back to his own home, while his wife stayed in Tin-muth.

When it was time to bring the wheat in from the field, Sam-son went down to see his wife, and took with him a young kid. But when he came to the house her fath-er would not let him go in, and told him that she was his wife no more, but had gone to live with some one else. Then Sam-son was in a great rage, and he went and caught more than ten score fox-es, and set bits of wood on fire, and tied these fire-brands to their tails, and let them loose in the fields and vine-yards of the Phil-is-tines.

And they set fire to the grain, and burnt it all up.

And the grape-vines and fruit trees were burnt, and much harm was done.

When the Phil-is-tines found out that it was Sam-son who had done this they took his wife and her fath-er and burnt them to death. And Sam-son fought and slew a host of the Phil-is-tines, and then went on the top of a high rock called E-tam to stay there.

Then a crowd of men went up with a rush to the top of the rock, and they said to Sam-son, We have come to bind thee, that we may give thee in-to the hands of the Phil-is-tines.

Sam-son made them swear that they would not put him to death, and they bound him with strong cords and brought him down from the rock.

As they drew near the camp of the Phil-is-tines a great shout went up from the men there. And the Lord gave Sam-son such strength that he broke the cords from his arms as if they had been burnt threads.

And Sam-son took up the jaw-bone of an ass, and with it he fought the Phil-is-tines and slew a host of them.

**SAM-SON SLAY-ING THE PHIL-IS-TINES.**

Then a great thirst came on him, and there was no well near from which he could drink. And he grew so weak that he cried out to the Lord not to let him die of thirst or fall in-to the hands of his foes.

And the Lord made a spring at that place and wa-ter ran out, and when Sam-son had drunk, his strength came back to him.

Sam-son came to the town of Ga-za, and went in a house there. Now the Phil-is-tines dwelt in Ga-za, and when they heard that Sam-son was there they shut the gates of the town, and kept watch near them all night. They said when the day dawns we will kill him.

But in the dead of the night Sam-son rose up and came to the gates of the town, and when he found them shut he took them up—posts, bar and all—and bore them a long way off to the top of a hill.

Sam-son's hair had not been cut, and it had grown thick and long. And there was a wo-man named De-li-lah whom Sam-son used to go and see. And when the Phil-is-tines heard of it they came to her and told her if she would find out how they might bind Sam-son and bear him off, they would give her a large sum of gold.

So when Sam-son came to De-li-lah's house she said to him, Tell me, I pray thee what makes thee so strong, and with what thou couldst be bound and not break loose?

Sam-son said if they bound him with sev-en green withes—that is, cords made out of soft twigs—he would be so weak that he could not break them.

When De-li-lah told this to the Phil-is-tines they brought her sev-en green withes, and Sam-son let her bind him with them. Now she had men hid in her house who were to take Sam-son if he could not break the twigs. And when she had bound him she cried out, The Phil-is-tines seize thee, Sam-son! And as soon as she had said these words he broke the green withes as if they were burnt threads.

Then De-li-lah knew that Sam-son made fun of her and told her lies, and she said once more, Tell me, I pray thee, with what thou canst be bound and not break loose.

**SAM-SON CAR-RY-ING THE GATES OF GA-ZA.**

Sam-son told her if he were bound with new ropes, which had not been used, that his strength would leave him, and he would be too weak to break them.

So she took new ropes and bound him. But ere the men who were hid in the room could spring out and take him, Sam-son broke the ropes from his arms as if they had been threads.

Then De-li-lah told Sam-son that he did but mock her and tell her lies, and she begged him to let her know how he might be bound.

And he said if she would weave his hair with the web in the loom his strength would go from him. And she wove his long hair in with the web, and made it fast with a large peg that was part of the loom.

Then she cried out, and Sam-son rose up and went off with the great peg, and the whole of the web that was in the loom.

Then she said he did not love her or he would not make sport of her in this way. And she teased him each day, and gave him no peace, so that at last he had to tell her the truth.

He said his hair had not been cut since he was born, and if it were shaved off he would lose all his strength.

It was wrong for Sam-son to tell her this, for she was bad at heart and not a true friend. But he did not know then how great was his sin.

De-li-lah knew that this time Sam-son had told her the truth; so she sent for the Phil-is-tines to come up to her house.

Then while Sam-son slept, she had a man come in and shave all the hair from his head. And when this was done she cried out, The Phil-is-tines seize thee, Sam-son.

## SAM-SON AND DE-LI-LAH.

And he woke from his sleep, and knew not his strength had gone from him.

Then the Phil-is-tines took him and put out his eyes, brought him down to Ga-za, and bound him with chains of brass. And they made him fast to a mill-stone, and he had to work hard to grind their corn.

While he was shut up in jail Sam-son had time to think of his sins, and he no doubt cried out to the Lord to keep him. For his hair grew out and his strength came back. But the Phil-is-tines did not know this.

They had made their own god, and its name was Da-gon. And they thought that Da-gon gave Sam-son in-to their hands, and loud was their praise of him. And all the Phil-is-tines met in the large house that had been built for Da-gon that they might bow down to their god and give him thanks.

The crowd was great, and their hearts were full of joy. And they said, Send for Sam-son that he may make sport for us. And poor blind Sam-son was brought in, and sat down in their midst. And those in the house and those on the roof made sport of him in all sorts of ways.

And Sam-son put his arms round two of the great posts that held up the house. And he bent down, and the house fell, and most of the Phil-is-tines were killed. Sam-son died with them, and by his death slew more of the foes of Is-ra-el than he had slain in all his life.

**SAM-SON DE-STROYS THE TEM-PLE.**

# CHAPTER X.

## RUTH.

WHILE Is-ra-el was ruled by a judge whose name has not come down to us, a dearth came on the land of Ca-naan. And one of the Jews who dwelt in Beth-le-hem, took his wife and his two sons and went to stay for a while in the land of Mo-ab. His wife's name was Na-o-mi. The man died while they were in Mo-ab, and in a few years each of the sons took him a wife. And their names were Or-pah and Ruth. At the end of ten years the sons died, and Na-o-mi and their wives dwelt in the land of Mo-ab.

When Na-o-mi heard there was no lack of food in Is-ra-el, she made up her mind to go back to Beth-le-hem to live.

She told Or-pah and Ruth of her plan, and said if they choose to stay in the land of Mo-ab, where they were born, they might do so.

And they kissed her and wept and said they would go with her. But she bade them stay where they were, and at last Or-pah, with tears in her eyes, kissed Na-o-mi good-bye and went back to her own home. But Ruth would not leave her. She told Na-o-mi not to urge her to go, for nought but death should part them.

**RUTH AND NA-O-MI.**

So they went to the town of Beth-le-hem where Na-o-mi used to live.

It was the days when the grain was ripe in the fields, and the men had gone out to cut it down.

And Na-o-mi had a kins-man in Beth-le-hem, whose name was Bo-az, and he was a rich and great man. And Ruth said to Na-o-mi, Let me now go to the fields and glean the ears of corn.

To glean is to pick up. And poor folks, who had no fields of their own, went to pick up that which was left on the ground for them.

**RUTH.**

And Na-o-mi told Ruth to go. And she went out and came to the field that was owned by the rich man, Bo-az.

When Bo-az saw Ruth he asked the men who she was, and where she came from. And one of them said, She came with Na-o-mi from the land of Mo-ab. And she said to us, I pray you let me glean where the field has been reaped. And we told her she might, and she has been there for some hours. Then Bo-az went to Ruth.

So she went out each day to his field, and gleaned there till the grain was all cut and in the barns.

Na-o-mi said to Ruth, Bo-az will win-now the bar-ley to-night. To win-now is to fan, or to drive off by means of a wind. The grain was first threshed, then thrown from the hands up in the air. The wind would blow off the chaff and the good grain would fall to the ground.

## BO-AZ AND RUTH.

Na-o-mi told Ruth to go in and speak to Bo-az the things she told her. So Ruth did as Na-o-mi said, and went down to the fields where Bo-az and his men were.

When she came back to Na-o-mi she told her all that she had said and done.

The next day Bo-az went down to the gate of Beth-le-hem, and told all the chief men whom he met there that he meant to make Ruth his wife. And the men said they would make it known, and prayed the Lord would bless Ruth and add to the fame and wealth of the rich and great Bo-az.

So Bo-az took Ruth for his wife. And they had a son O-bed. And Na-o-mi was its nurse.

# CHAPTER XI.

## JOB.

THERE was a man in the land of Uz whose name was Job. He was a good man and tried to do all that was right in the sight of the Lord. And God gave him ten chil-dren: sev-en boys and three girls. He gave Job great wealth, too, so that there was no man in all that part of the world as rich as he was.

When Job's sons were grown up and had homes of their own, they used to make feasts in turn, and send for their three sis-ters to come and eat and drink with them. And Job kept them in mind of all they owed to God, and urged them to lead good and true lives, and to do no wrong.

When Job had lived at his ease and been a rich man for a long term of years, a great change took place. He lost all his wealth, and all his chil-dren; for it was God's will to try him and see how he would bear these ills.

One day one of his men came to him in great haste, and said, While we were in the field with the ploughs, a band of thieves came and drove off the ox-en and ass-es and slew thy men who were with them, and I a-lone am left to tell thee.

While this man spoke, there came up one who said, A great fire has come down from the sky and burnt up thy sheep, and all those who took care of them, and I a-lone am left to tell thee.

While he yet spoke, a third man came and said, Thy foes came and took all thy cam-els, and slew the men who had charge of them, and I a-lone am left to tell thee.

Then a fourth came, and said, Thy chil-dren were at a feast in the house of thy first-born son, when there came a great wind that broke down the house, and it fell on the young men and they are all dead, and I a-lone am left to tell thee.

When Job heard these things he tore his clothes, and bowed down to the earth, as if at the feet of God. And he said, I had nought when I came in-to the world, and I shall have nought when I die and go out of it. God gave me all that I had, and God took it from me. He knows what is best for me, and I thank him for all that he has done. So Job did not sin, nor speak ill of God, though his grief was so great and had come up-on him in such a strange, swift way.

To try Job still more, God let him get sick and he was in great pain. Boils came on him and from head to foot he was a mass of sores.

Then his wife came to Job and said, Dost thou still trust God? Do so no more, but curse him, though he kill thee for it.

Job said, Thou dost not speak wise words. When we have so much good from God, shall we not be con-tent to take our share of the ills he may send? In all this Job said not a word that was wrong.

Now Job had three friends, who, when they heard of his hard lot, came to talk with him and cheer him. But when they saw him, the change was so great they did not know him.

Then they rent their clothes and wept, and sat down on the ground near him, but did not speak for some time, for they could see that his grief was great. These friends thought that Job must have done some great sin, else these ills would not have been sent up-on him. When they spoke to him they said, If thou hast done wrong, do so no more, and God will free thee from thy pains.

**JOB, AND HIS FRIENDS.**

Now Job knew that he had done no wrong, and he said to them, You came to soothe me, but what you say does not soothe me at all. Did I send for you, or ask you to help me? If you were in such grief as I am, I might say hard things of you and call you bad men. But I would not do so; but would speak kind words to you, and try to help you bear your ills, and to make your grief less.

Then Job spoke of his own griefs, and said: O, that the Lord would put me to death that I might suf-fer no more. When I lie down at night I can-not sleep, but toss on my bed in pain and wish the day would dawn. Or, if I fall a-sleep for a while, I have the worst kind of dreams, so that I would be glad to die and wake no more in this world. O, that I had some one to speak to God for me, for he does not hear when I pray. Yet I know that he lives who will save my soul, and that he will come on the earth, and I shall rise up from my grave and see God for my-self.

But when Job found that he could not die, nor be made well, but must still bear his pains, he grew cross, and was not at all like the Job of old. He found fault, and said that his griefs were too great, and that God was not kind to put him in such pain.

His three friends did not try to calm him, or to cheer him with the hope that his woes would soon be at an end, nor did they bid him trust in God and seek help and strength from him. But they told him that he must have done some great wrong, else God would not have sent all these ills up-on him.

This did not please Job, and he spoke to them in great wrath, and they spoke back in the same style.

When they had talked in this way for some time, and had each of them said things they ought not to have said, they heard a voice speak to them out of a whirl-wind that swept by the place. It was the voice of God.

And the voice spoke to Job and told him of the great works that God had done; that it was he who made the earth, the sea, and the sky. He sends the rain on the field to make the grass grow and the flow-ers to spring up. He sends the cold and the heat, the frost and the snow, and the ice that stops the flow of the streams. He sends the clouds, and the roar and the flash that come from them when the storms rage. He made the horse that is so swift and strong, and has no fear in time of war, but will rush in-to the fight at the sound of the trump.

All this and more the voice spoke from the whirl-wind. And when God had told Job of all these great works, he asked him if he could do these things, or if he thought he was so wise that he could teach God what it was best to do.

Then Job saw what a sin it was to find fault with God. And he was full of shame, and said: My guilt is great; I spoke of that of which I knew naught, and I bow down in the dust be-fore thee.

God said to Job's three friends, I am wroth with you, for you did not speak in the right way to Job. Now, lest I pun-ish you, take sev-en young bulls and sev-en rams and burn them on the al-tar, and ask Job to pray for you, for him will I hear. So they did as the Lord told them, and Job prayed for them, and God for-gave them their sins.

In a short time Job was well once more. His pains all left him; and then his friends and all his folks came to see him and they had a good feast. And each man brought him a rich gift, and the Lord blest him more than he had done be-fore, and gave him twice as much wealth. He had great herds of sheep, and cam-els, and ox-en and ass-es, and large fields for them to roam in, and a host of men to care for them. So that he was a great man once more.

And God gave him ten chil-dren: sev-en boys and three girls. And when these girls grew up, there were no maids in all the land so fair as they in face and form. And Job had great peace of mind, and dwelt at his ease for long, long years; and when he died he was an old, old man.

# CHAPTER XII.

## SAMUEL, THE CHILD OF GOD.

THERE was a man of Is-ra-el who went up each year from the town of Ra-mah to a place called Shi-loh to pay his vows to the Lord of hosts. And his wife, whose name was Han-nah, went with him. The man's name was El-ka-nah.

**SAM-U-EL.**

E-li was the high-priest at that time, and as he sat in the Lord's house he saw Han-nah on her knees with her eyes full of tears.

And he spoke to her in a kind voice, and said: May God grant thee what thou dost ask of him. And Han-nah was glad at the high-priest's words, for she had asked God to give her a son.

And the Lord gave Han-nah a son, and she called his name Sam-u-el, which means "Asked of the Lord."

Sam-u-el was quite young when Han-nah took him up to the house of the Lord at Shi-loh. And when they brought the child to E-li, Han-nah said, I am the wo-man that stood by thee here and prayed to the Lord. For this child did I pray, and the Lord heard me and gave me what I asked for. So I have brought him to the Lord; so long as he lives shall he be the child of God. For this was the vow she made if God would give her a son.

And Sam-u-el was left to stay with E-li in the Lord's house.

Now E-li had two sons, and they were priests in the Lord's house. But they were not fit for the place, for they were bad men, and broke God's laws. And by their sins they kept men from the house of the Lord.

But Sam-u-el, though a young child, did what was right and pleased the Lord. And his moth-er made him a coat, and brought it to him each year when she and her hus-band went up to Shi-loh. And E-li spoke kind words to them, and asked the Lord to bless them for the sake of the child whom they gave to him.

Now E-li was an old man, and when he heard of all the things his sons had done, he did not drive them out of the Lord's house as he should have done, but let them go on in their sins. He cared more to please his sons than he did to please the Lord.

**HAN-NAH PRE-SENTS SAM-U-EL TO E-LI.**

One night when E-li and Sam-u-el lay down to sleep, the child heard a voice speak his name. And he said, Here am I. And he got up and ran to E-li, for he thought it was his voice, and he said, Here am I, for thou did'st call me.

E-li said, I did not call thee, my son. Go back, and lie down. And the lad did so.

In a short time he heard the same voice say, Sam-u-el—Sam-u-el.

And he rose at once and went to E-li, and said to him, Here am I, for thou did'st call me. But E-li said, I did not call thee, and sent the lad back to his bed once more.

Then Sam-u-el heard the voice a third time, and went to E-li and said, Here am I, for thou did'st call me.

And E-li knew it was the Lord who spoke to Sam-u-el. And he said to the lad, Go, lie down, and if he call thee, say, Speak, Lord, for I hear thee.

And Sam-u-el went and lay down. And the Lord came for the fourth time, and called, Sam-u-el—Sam-u-el!

And Sam-u-el said, Speak, Lord, for I hear thee.

And the Lord told Sam-u-el all that he meant to do to the house of E-li. He had let his sons go on in their sins, and they were to be put to death in a way that would make men fear God.

Sam-u-el lay still till day-light. Then he rose, but did not dare to tell E-li what God had told him.

But E-li called him and said, What did the Lord say to thee? I pray thee hide it not from me.

So Sam-u-el told E-li all that the Lord had said. When E-li heard it, he said, It is the Lord, let him do what he thinks is best.

And Sam-u-el grew, and the Lord was with him and blest him, and it was known to all that he was one of God's saints, who could fore-tell things that were to take place. Such wise men were some-times called seers.

The words which God spoke to Sam-u-el came true; for the chil-dren of Is-ra-el went out to fight the Phil-is-tines, and a host of them were slain.

Those who came back said, Let us take the ark out with us to save us from our foes.

## CAP-TURE OF THE ARK.

Now God had not told them to take the ark, and it was a sin for them to touch it. They should have put their trust in the Lord, and looked to him for help.

But they sent to Shi-loh for the ark, and E-li's two sons came with it. When it was brought to the camp the Jews gave such a shout that the earth shook with the noise.

And when the Phil-is-tines heard it, they said, What does it mean? And they were told that the ark of the Lord had been brought to the camp of Is-ra-el.

And they were in great fear; for they said, God is come to the camp! Woe un-to us, for this is the first time such a thing has been done!

And they said, Let us be strong and fight like men, that we may not be slaves to these Jews!

So they fought once more with the Jews, and slew a host of them, and the rest fled to their tents. And the ark of the Lord fell in-to the hands of the foe, and E-li's two sons were slain.

And the same day a man ran down to Shi-loh, with his clothes rent, and bits of earth on his head to show his grief.

E-li sat on a seat by the way-side, where he kept watch, for he was in great fear lest harm should come to the ark of God. And when the man came through the crowd and told that the ark was lost, all cried out with great fear. And when E-li heard the noise, he said, What is it? What do those sounds mean? For his eyes were dim with age, and he could not see.

And the man ran up to E-li and said, I am he that came out of the fight, and I fled from there to-day.

And E-li said, What word hast thou, my son?

**THE RE-TURN OF THE ARK.**

And he said that Is-ra-el had been put to flight with great loss, his two sons were dead, and the ark of God in the hands of the Phil-is-tines.

When the man spoke of the ark of God, E-li fell off the seat by the side of the gate, and broke his neck, and died there. And he had been a high priest and a judge in Is-ra-el for two-score years.

And the ark of God was with the Phil-is-tines for more than half the year, and to each place where it was sent it brought great grief.

So at last they sent for their wise men, and said to them, What shall we do with the ark of the Lord? To what place shall we send it?

And the wise men told them to make a new cart, and tie two cows to it, but to bring the calves home with them. Then they should put the ark on the cart, and let the cows draw it where they would.

If the cows should leave their calves and go down to the land of Is-ra-el, it would be a sign that the Lord was their guide, and that he had sent these ills on the Phil-is-tines for their great sins.

But if the cows did not take the ark, it would show that the Lord did not want it back, and that all these ills they had to bear had come by chance, and were not sent from the Lord.

So the Phil-is-tines did as their wise men said. They took the two cows and tied them to the cart, and shut up their calves at home. And they laid the ark on the cart, and let the cows go where they chose.

And the cows took the straight road to the land of Is-ra-el till they came to a place called Beth-she-mesh.

The Jews who dwelt there were out in the wheat fields. And the cows brought the cart to the fields of a man named Josh-u-a, and stood there by a great stone.

Then some of the men of Le-vi came and took the ark and set it on the stone. And they broke up the cart, and burnt the cows as a gift of praise to the Lord.

# CHAPTER XIII.

## SAMUEL THE MAN OF GOD.

WHEN E-li died, Sam-u-el was made a judge in Is-ra-el. And he went from place to place to teach men the law. And as the ark had not been brought back to Shi-loh, Sam-u-el built an al-tar in his own house and served God there.

The chil-dren of Is-ra-el set up strange gods, and the Phil-is-tines went to war with them. And Sam-u-el told them to give up their false gods and serve the Lord, and he would save them from their foes. And they did so. And he said, Come up to Miz-peh, and I will pray to the Lord for you.

And they came to Miz-peh, and gave their hearts to the Lord, and were in grief for their sins.

And when the Phil-is-tines heard they were at Miz-peh, they went up to fight them. And the chil-dren of Is-ra-el were in great fear, and Sam-u-el plead for them, and when the fight came on the Lord sent a fierce storm that put the Phil-is-tines to flight, and they fled from the field with great loss.

And Sam-u-el set up a stone at Miz-peh, and gave it the name of Eb-en-e-zer—"The Stone of Help."

When Sam-u-el was an old man he set his two sons to judge Is-ra-el. But his sons were not just men, and did not rule as their fath-er had done. If a man did wrong, they would say it was right if he paid them for it. And the wise men came to Sam-u-el, and said to him, As thou art old, and thy sons walk not in thy ways, make us a king to judge us.

Sam-u-el felt hurt when they asked him to choose a king, and asked the Lord to tell him what to do.

And the Lord told Sam-u-el to choose a king for them.

Now there was a man whose name was Kish, and he had a son whose name was Saul, a tall young man of fine form and good looks.

And the ass-es of Kish were lost. And he said to Saul, his son, Take one of the men with you, and go find the ass-es.

And they went a long way and could not find them. And Saul said to the man with him, Come, let us go back, lest my fath-er think we are lost.

## THE STONE OF HELP.

And the man said to Saul, There is a man of God here, and what he says is sure to come to pass. It may be that he can tell us what we ought to do Saul said, Thy word is good; come, let us go. And they went to the town where Sam-u-el, the man of God, was. And they met him on their way.

And the Lord made it known to Sam-u-el that this was the man he should choose to reign in Is-ra-el.

And Saul drew near to Sam-u-el, and said, Tell me, I pray thee, where the seer's house is.

And Sam-u-el said, I am the seer; and the ass-es that were lost are found. And he took Saul and his man to his own house, and made them spend the night there.

The next day Sam-u-el took Saul to the roof of his house, and had a talk with him.

Then they went out on the street, and as they drew near the gate of the town, Sam-u-el said to Saul, Bid thy man pass on, but do thou stand still for a while, that I may show thee the word of God.

Then Sam-u-el took a horn of oil and poured it on Saul's head.

This was done when a man was made a high-priest; and the same thing was done when he was made a king. And God was pleased with Saul, and gave him a new heart; but as yet none but these two knew that Saul was to be King of the Jews.

Sam-u-el spoke to the chil-dren of Is-ra-el and told them once more all that the Lord had done for them, how he had brought them out of the land of E-gypt, and set them free from their foes, and yet they would not serve the Lord, but cried out for a king. So he bade them all go up to Miz-peh that the Lord might choose them a king.

**SAUL IN HIS HID-ING PLACE.**

And the Lord chose Saul. But when the men went to seek for him, they could not find him. And the Lord said, He hath hid in the midst of the stuff. And they ran and brought him out, and he was so tall that all the rest had to look up to him.

And Sam-u-el said, This is he whom the Lord hath sent to rule thee. There is none like him, as thou canst see.

And they all cried out, God save the king! Then Sam-u-el told them what they were to do, and how the king was to rule, and wrote it down in a book.

When Saul had been king for two years, he set out with his son, Jon-a-than, to fight the Phil-is-tines. And a great host went with them. And the Phil-is-tines had more men than they could count. And when the Jews saw the strength of their foes, they were in great fear, and ran and hid in caves and pits, or fled to the high hills where the rocks would screen them. So there were but few left to go out with Saul, and they shook with dread.

And Saul came to Gil-gal, where he was to meet Sam-u-el, but he was not there. Sam-u-el had told him to wait for him, and he would tell him what he was to do.

But at the end of a week Saul had the flesh brought to him and laid on the stone, and he set fire to it, that the flame might rise to God and bring peace to the land. And as soon as Saul had done this thing, Sam-u-el came. And Saul went out to meet him, that he might bless him.

And Sam-u-el said, What hast thou done?

And Saul told of the strait he was in, and that the Phil-is-tines were near in great force, and said that when Sam-u-el did not come he felt that he must send up a plea to God for aid in this hour.

Sam-u-el told him that he had done wrong. When the Lord told him to wait, he should wait. And now his reign would be a short one, and God would choose a new king to take his place.

In those days men fought with bows and ar-rows. And while the Jews were held as slaves by the Phil-is-tines they would not let them have swords or spears, lest they should rise up and kill them.

And they sent all the smiths out of the land, lest they should make these things for the chil-dren of Is-ra-el.

So when they went out to fight none of them had a sword or a spear but Saul and his son.

In those days men wore coats of mail, and bore a shield with them so as to ward off the darts. These shields were made of a thick piece of wood, on which the skin of an ox was stretched when dried.

Jon-a-than, Saul's son, wore a coat of mail, and had a man to bear his spear and his shield when he did not care to use them. And he said to his man, Come, let us go to the camp of the Phil-is-tines. For it may be that the Lord will help us.

And the man said he would go.

Jon-a-than said this should be their sign: They would go where the foe could see them, and if they said, Wait there till I come to you, they would know the Lord did not mean to help them. But if the Phil-is-tines said, Come up to us and we will show you some-thing, they would go up, for the Lord would be with them.

So Jon-a-than and his man stood out where the foe could see them. And the Phil-is-tines made sport of them, and cried out, Come up to us, and we will shew you some-thing.

And the two went up the rocks on their hands and feet, and fought with the Phil-is-tines, and slew a score of them. And the Lord shook the earth, so that the Phil-is-tines were in great fear.

Now Saul and the men who were with him did not know what his son had done. But his watch-man, who was on the look-out, saw that there was a fight in the camp of the Phil-is-tines, and told Saul of it.

And Saul and his men went to join in the fight. And all those who had hid in caves and holes, or up on the mount, when they heard that the Phil-is-tines had fled, went with Saul, and Is-ra-el won the day.

But Saul did not de-sire to please the Lord in all things. For when the Lord sent him out to fight King A-gag, he told Saul to wipe him and all he had from the face of the earth. But Saul kept back some of the spoils, the best of the sheep and lambs, and did not put the king to death as he should have done.

And the Lord told Sam-u-el that Saul was not a good king, and his reign should be short.

And it made Sam-u-el sad to hear this, and he prayed to God all night. Then he had a talk with Saul, who did not look at his sins in the right light. And Sam-u-el told him that his reign as king would soon be at an end.

**DA-VID A-NOINT-ED BY SAM-U-EL.**

God told Sam-u-el not to mourn for Saul, but to go down to Beth-le-hem, to the house of a man named Jes-se, one of whose sons was to be made king. And the Lord said he was not to look for one with a fine face or form. For the Lord sees not as man sees, and he looks on the heart.

So he went down to Beth-le-hem, and did as the Lord told him. And Jes-se had his sev-en sons pass one by one be-fore Sam-u-el. And Sam-u-el thought that the first-born must be the one whom God chose to be king. But the Lord told him he was not the one. And they all went by, and not one of them was the one on whom God had set his seal.

And Sam-u-el said to Jes-se, Are these all thy sons?

And Jes-se said, No there is yet one left; but he is quite a lad, and is now in the field where he cares for the sheep.

And Sam-u-el told Jes-se to send for him at once. And Jes-se sent for him, and he was brought in, and his cheeks were red, and his eyes bright. And the Lord said to Sam-u-el, Rise—for this is he.

And Sam-u-el rose, and took the horn of oil and poured it on the young man's head. So the Lord chose Da-vid to be king when Saul should be put out of the way.

And Da-vid felt a great change in his heart, for the Lord was there to make him strong and wise, and fit for the high place he was to fill.

But there was no peace in Saul's heart, and his mind was ill at ease.

And his men said it might soothe him to have some one play on the harp. For sweet sounds will some-times calm the mind.

So Saul said, Find a man who can play well on the harp, and bring him to me.

And one of them said that he knew such a man. He was the son of Jes-se, who dwelt at Beth-le-hem, and his name was Da-vid.

And Saul sent men to Jes-se and told him to send Da-vid, his son, who kept the sheep.

And Da-vid came to Saul, and stayed with him to wait on him. And when Saul was sad and ill at ease, Da-vid would take his harp and play for him, and he would soon be well.

# CHAPTER XIV.

## DAVID AND SAUL.

WHILE Saul was yet king, the Phil-is-tines came forth once more to fight the chil-dren of Is-ra-el. And Saul and his men went out to meet them. There were two high hills on each side of a deep vale, and from these two hills the foe-men fought.

The Phil-is-tines had on their side a man who was more than ten feet high. He wore a coat of mail, and was bound with brass from head to foot, so that no sword or spear could wound him.

And he cried out to Saul's men, Choose a man from your midst and let him come down to me. If he can fight with me and kill me, then we will be your slaves. But if I kill him then you must serve us. I dare you to send a man to fight with me.

When Saul and his men heard these words they were in great fear, for there was no one in their ranks who would dare fight with such a gi-ant.

And each morn and eve, for more than a month, this great man, whose name was Go-li-ath, drew near Saul and his troops and dared them to send a man out to fight him.

Now when the war broke out three of Jes-se's sons went with Saul, but Da-vid went back to Beth-le-hem to feed sheep.

And Jes-se said to Da-vid, Take this parched corn and these ten loaves of bread, and run down to camp and bring me back word how thy broth-ers are.

And Da-vid rose up the next morn, and found some one to take care of his sheep, and went as his fath-er told him.

And he came to the camp just as the men were on their way to the fight, and the air was filled with their shouts.

And he left the goods he had brought in the care of a man, and ran in the midst of the troops, and spoke to his three broth-ers.

And while he stood there, Go-li-ath came out from the ranks of the Phil-is-tines, and dared some one to fight with him.

And Da-vid heard his words. And the men of Is-ra-el fled from his face. And Da-vid heard them speak of what would be done to the man who should kill him; for the king would give him great wealth, and set him in a high place.

And Da-vid spoke to the men near him, and made use of strong words.

And his broth-ers told him to go home and take care of his sheep, for it was just a trick of his to come up to camp that he might see the fight.

**DA-VID BE-FORE SAUL.**

Da-vid said, I have done no wrong! and the men to whom he spoke went and told Saul what he had said. And Saul sent for him, but did not know that he was the same one who used to play on the harp for him.

And Da-vid told Saul he would go out and fight the great man from Gath. And Saul said, Thou art but a youth, and he has been a man of war all his days.

Then Da-vid told Saul how he had fought with and slain the wild beasts that came out of the woods to eat up the lambs of his flock. And, said he, this man is no more than a wild beast, and the Lord will save me from him as he did from the paw of the li-on and the bear.

And Saul said, Go, and the Lord go with thee. And Saul put on him a coat of mail, and clothed him in brass from head to foot, and hung a sword at his side. But Da-vid took them all off, and said, I have not tried them, and can-not use them.

And he took his staff in his hand, and chose five smooth stones from the brook and put them in a bag that he wore. And his sling was in his hand when he drew near to Go-li-ath.

Go-li-ath came near to Da-vid, and when he saw what a youth he was, he drew up his head with great scorn.

Da-vid ran to meet him, and put his hand in his bag and drew forth a stone, and slung it, and struck Go-li-ath on the fore-head with such force that the stone sank in through the bone and he fell on his face to the earth.

**DA-VID WITH GO-LI-ATH'S HEAD.**

Then Da-vid ran and stood on Go-li-ath, and drew his sword from its sheath, and slew him and cut off his head.

And when the Phil-is-tines saw that the man in whom they had put their trust was dead they fled.

And Da-vid came back from the fight with the head of Go-li-ath in his hand, and was brought to Saul.

And Saul would not let Da-vid go back to his own home, but made him stay with him. And Jon-a-than fell in love with him, and to show his love, took off all the rich clothes he had on and put them on Da-vid, and gave him his sword, his bow, and his belt. And Da-vid did as Saul told him, and all who saw him were pleased with him, and Saul put him at the head of his men of war.

But when King Saul and his men went through the towns on their way back from the fight, the folks came out and sang and danced to praise them for what they had done.

But they said more in praise of Da-vid than of Saul, and when Saul heard it he was wroth, and from that day ceased to be Da-vid's friend.

The next day Da-vid stood near Saul with his harp in his hand to play him some sweet tunes.
 And Saul held a spear in his hand, and he cast it at Da-vid so that it would go through him and pin him to the wall. But Da-vid saw it and took a step one side, and it did him no harm.

Twice was this done, and when Saul found that he could not hurt Da-vid, he was in great fear of him, for he knew the Lord was with him. So he drove Da-vid from his house, and sent men to lay in wait to kill him.

**JON-A-THAN AND DA-VID.**

But Da-vid fled from them and ran to the place where Jon-a-than was, and said to him, What have I done that the king seeks my life?

Now Jon-a-than did not know that the king meant to kill Da-vid, so he said to him, Thou shalt not die. My fath-er would have told me if he meant to kill thee. But Da-vid said it was true.

The next day was to be a feast day, and the king would look for Dav-id to come and eat with him. But Da-vid was in such fear of Saul that he did not care to go, and begged Jon-a-than to let him hide him-self for three days. If the king asks where I am, said Da-vid, tell him that thou did'st give me leave to go home.

Jon-a-than told Da-vid that at the end of the three days he should come and hide in the field near a rock that was there. And Jon-a-than said he would shoot three ar-rows as if he took aim at a mark. And he would send a lad out to pick them up. And if he said to the lad, Go, find them, they are on this side of thee, then Da-vid might know that all was at peace and the king would do him no harm. But if he should cry out that the darts were be-yond the lad, then Da-vid would know that he must flee, for the king meant to do him harm.

So Da-vid hid him-self in the field; and when the feast day came Saul sat down to eat with his back to the wall. And he saw that Da-vid was not in his place, but said not a word. The next day when he found Da-vid was not in his place, Saul said to his son, Why comes not Da-vid to eat these two days?

Jon-a-than said that Da-vid pled so hard for leave to go home to his own folks, that he had told him to go, and that was why he was not at the feast.

Then Saul was in a great rage, and said to his son, As long as Da-vid lives thou canst not be a king. Send for him, and bring him here that he may be put to death.

And Jon-a-than said, Why should he be slain? What hath he done?

**JON-A-THAN SHOOT-ING THE AR-ROWS.**

Saul threw his spear at Jon-a-than. And the young man knew by this that the king meant to kill Da-vid. So the next morn the king's son went out to the field, and took a lad with him. And he said, Run now, and pick up the ar-rows that I shoot.

And as he ran, Jon-a-than sent a dart o'er his head; and when the lad came to the place where it fell, the king's son cried out, It is be-yond thee. Make haste, and stay not.

Da-vid heard these words and knew that he must flee, for if Saul caught him he would kill him.

The lad brought the darts to Jon-a-than, and did not know why the king's son had shot them and called out to him as he did. And Jon-a-than gave him his bow and ar-rows, and sent him back to town with them.

As soon as the lad was gone, Da-vid came out from the place where he was hid, and fell on his face to the ground, and bowed three times. Then he rose and threw his arms round Jon-a-than's neck, and the two friends wept as if their hearts would break.

Then Da-vid fled from Saul, and hid in the woods and caves.

Saul went out with a large force of men to seek Da-vid on the rocks where the wild goats fed. And Saul came to a cave, and went in to lie down and rest.

Da-vid and his men were in the cave, but Saul could not see them. And the men wished to kill Saul; but Da-vid would not let them. While he was there Da-vid stole up to Saul and cut off a piece of his robe. And Saul did not know it.

**DA-VID AND SAUL.**

When Saul went out of the cave, Da-vid went out af-ter him and cried out, My lord and my king!

And when Saul looked back, Da-vid bowed down to him with his face to the earth. And he told Saul to pay no heed to those who said he meant to harm the king. For if he had sought to kill Saul he might have done so that day while he was in the cave. And Da-vid showed Saul the piece of his robe he had cut off.

And some bade me kill thee, said Da-vid, but I would not, for thou art my lord and my king. Then Da-vid held up the piece of cloth he had cut from Saul's robe, and said, Since I was so near thee as to cut this off and did not kill thee, thou may'st know that I have no wish to harm thee. Yet thou dost hunt for me to kill me. Let the Lord judge 'twixt thee and me, and save me from thy hand, and save thee as he will, for I will not harm thee.

When Saul heard Da-vid speak thus, all hate went out of his heart, and he wept as he said, Thou hast done good to me for the wrongs I did thee, and may the Lord bless thee for it. Now I know that thou wilt some day be the king of Is-ra-el.

And Saul went home, and Da-vid and his men went back to the cave.

But Da-vid knew that he could not trust Saul, so he fled to the land of the Phil-is-tines, and he and his men dwelt there in the town of Gath for the space of a year and four months.

**DA-VID TAKES GO-LI-ATH'S SWORD.**

While he was there, the Phil-is-tines went out to fight with Saul once more, and when he saw what a host of them there was, his heart shook with fear. He asked the Lord what he should do, but the Lord did not come to him in dreams, or speak one word to him.

Sam-u-el was dead, and the Lord had said it was a sin to go to a witch, or a seer, to find out the things that would take place, and Saul had sent all these folks out of the land.

But now he was in such a strait that he felt he must have help of some sort. And one of his men told him there was at En-dor a witch who could work strange charms, and fore-tell what was to take place. So the king drest himself so that he would not be known, and went at night with two of his men to see the witch of En-dor. And he said to her, Bring me up him whom I shall name to thee.

And the witch said to him, Dost thou not know that Saul has sent all those that work charms out of the land? And why dost thou set a snare for my life, so that I will be put to death?

And Saul said, As the Lord lives there shall no harm come to thee for this thing.

Then the witch said, Whom shall I bring up to thee? And he said, Bring me Sam-u-el.

So the witch made strange signs and spoke strange words, and swept her wand round and round. And when she saw the form of Sam-u-el rise up, she cried with a loud voice, Why did'st thou not tell me the truth? for thou art Saul!

And the king said, Have no fear. What did'st thou see?

And the witch said, I saw an old man with a cloak round him.

And Saul knew it was Sam-u-el, and bowed his face to the ground. And Sam-u-el said, Why hast thou brought me up? And Saul told him that he was in a great strait, that God had left him, and did not come to him in dreams or by the hand of wise men, and he thought that Sam-u-el might tell him what to do.

Sam-u-el said, Why then dost thou ask of me if the Lord hath left thee? He hath done to thee just as he said he would. Thy reign is at an end, and Da-vid shall rule in thy stead. And he told Saul that the next day he and his sons would be dead, and Is-ra-el in the hands of the foes.

When Saul heard these words he fell down in a swoon, for he had had no food for a day and a night.

And the witch brought bread and bade him eat, that he might have strength to go on his way. And Saul and his men ate of the food, and went their way that night.

Now the lords of the Phil-is-tines brought all their troops to a place called A-phek. And the king of Gath went there, and took Da-vid and his men with him. But the lords of the Phil-is-tines would not have the Jews in their midst lest they should turn on them and give them in-to the hands of king Saul.

So Da-vid and his men had to leave the camp, and the Phil-is-tines went out to fight, and the men of Is-ra-el fled from them with great loss. The king's three sons were slain, and an ar-row struck Saul and gave him a bad wound.

And Saul said to the man who bore his shield, Draw thy sword and put me to death. But the man did not dare to kill his king. So Saul took his own sword and fell on it, and thus died by his own hand. And when the man saw that Saul was dead, he fell on his sword and died with him.

And when it was known that Saul and his sons were dead, the Jews fled from that part of the land, and the Phil-is-tines went to live there.

In the course of a few years Da-vid was made king of Is-ra-el, and then went to live at Je-ru-sa-lem. He went to war, and took spoils of rich kings, and the Lord was with him, for he sought to do that which was right and just.

Da-vid had two sons: Sol-o-mon and Ab-sa-lom.

And in all the land there was no man with such a fine face and form as Ab-sa-lom, and he won much praise for his good looks. And he had a thick growth of long hair. But Ab-sa-lom had a bad heart, and his sins made Da-vid weep. But he did not scold Ab-sa-lom as he should have done, for the king was fond of his son, and so Ab-sa-lom went on from bad to worse.

He told what he would do when he was king, and made friends with those who thought it a fine thing to be on good terms with the king's son.

When he was two-score years of age, Ab-sa-lom said to the king, Let me, I pray thee, go up to Heb-ron to pay my vows.

And Da-vid told him to go. But it was not to serve the Lord that Ab-sa-lom went, but to have him-self made king in-stead of Da-vid. And he took ten score men with him, who did not know why or where they went, and sent spies all through the land to speak in his praise and urge that he be made king.

**DA-VID FOR-GIV-ING AB-SA-LOM.**

And when Da-vid heard of it he said to his men, Rise, let us flee from this place, lest Ab-sa-lom come and put us to death.

And they all fled from Je-ru-sa-lem, and went to hide in some lone place. And when Ab-sa-lom came to Je-ru-sa-lem he went to one of Da-vid's friends and asked him what he should do to be made king. A-hith-o-phel, who had once been a friend of Da-vid, and had now gone with the king's son, had said that he would go out with a large force and come up with Da-vid when he was weak and faint, so that he would be in a great fright. Those who were with Dav-id would flee, and he would soon put the king to death. Then, of course, Ab-sa-lom would be king.

But Ab-sa-lom would not do this till he had heard what Hu-sha-i said. Now Hu-sha-i was a true friend of Da-vid, and he told Ab-sa-lom to take more men than A-hith-o-phel had said, for he thought that would give Da-vid a chance to get out of the way. And Hu-sha-i sent two young men to tell Da-vid not to stop on the plains that night, but to cross the Jor-dan, lest he and all who were with him should be put to death.

But a boy saw the two sons of the high-priest who were on their way to Da-vid, and went and told Ab-sa-lom. And the priest's sons ran to a house near by, and hid in the well. And the wo-man who kept the house spread corn on top so that no one could see that a well was there.

And when Ab-sa-lom's men came in and asked the wo-man where the priest's sons were, she said they had gone on past the brook Ked-ron. And when the two could not be found the men went back.

Then the priest's sons came up out of the well, and made haste to give to Da-vid the word that Hu-sha-i had sent. And at dawn Da-vid and all his men crossed Jor-dan.

As soon as Ab-sa-lom had all the men he thought he would need, he set out to fight with Da-vid. And Da-vid drew up his men in line, and put Jo-ab at their head. And the king said, I will go out with you. But the men said he should not; so Da-vid staid by the gate and saw them go out to the fight, and bade them be kind to Ab-sa-lom for his sake.

**THE DEATH OF AB-SA-LOM.**

The fight took place in a wood. Ab-sa-lom rode on a mule, and as the mule passed 'neath a great oak, Ab-sa-lom's head caught in a branch, and he hung in mid air, while the mule went off down the road.

And a man saw it and told Jo-ab. And Jo-ab said, Why did'st thou not kill him? And the man said he would not kill the king's son, for he had heard Da-vid ask them to be kind to him.

But Jo-ab said, I can-not waste time with thee. And he took three darts in his hand and thrust them through Ab-sa-lom, so that he died. And he was thrown in-to a pit that was in the wood, and a great heap of stones was piled on him. And all the men who had been with him went back to their tents.

**DA-VID HEAR-ING OF AB-SA-LOM'S DEATH.**

Da-vid sat in the gate, and when men came back with news of the fight, he would ask of each one, Is Ab-sa-lom safe? And at last one of them said, May all the king's foes be as this young man is. Then Da-vid knew that Ab-sa-lom was dead, and he went to his own room and wept.

And he cried out with a loud voice, O, my son, Ab-sa-lom; my son, my son Ab-sa-lom! I would that God had let me die in thy stead, O, Ab-sa-lom, my son, my son!

Da-vid was king for two-score years, and was an old man when he died and had hosts of friends. And when he felt that his death was near, he bade his men take Sol-o-mon to a place called Gi-hon, and pour oil on his head. Then they were to blow the horn and cry out. God save King So-lo-mon.

And this was done; and when Da-vid died, Sol-o-mon sat on his throne and ruled Is-ra-el.

# CHAPTER XV.

## SOLOMON, THE WISE MAN.

SOL-O-MON gave his heart to God when he was young, and tried to lead a good life, and to do no wrong. And God spoke to him in a dream one night and said, Ask what I shall give thee.

And So-lo-mon said, Grant me, I pray thee a wise mind that I may know right from wrong, and judge well those who look up to me as their king.

This speech pleased the Lord, and he said, Since thou didst not ask me for great wealth, or for long life, or that thy foes might be put to death, I will make thee wise, and will give thee both great wealth and a long life if thou wilt serve me and keep my laws.

There came two wo-men to the king. And one of them said, My lord, I and this wo-man live in one house, and we each of us had a son. And this wo-man's child died in the night, and while I slept she came and took my child from me, and laid her own child by my side. And when I woke, and went to feed my child, it was dead. And I knew it was not my son.

It is your son.

It is not; the child that lives is mine.

The dead child is yours.

**THE JUDG-MENT OF SOL-O-MON.**

In this way they spoke, and the king heard them, and said, Bring me a sword! And a sword was brought to him.

And the king said, Cut the live child in two, and give half to one and half to the oth-er.

When the real moth-er of the child heard these words she cried out, O my lord, give her the child, but do not kill it.

But the oth-er said, Cut it in half, and let it not be hers or mine.

Then the king told his men to give the child to the one who tried to save its life, for he knew that she was the moth-er. And it was to find this out that he sent the men for the sword, and not to take the child's life.

**SHIPS OF SOL-O-MON.**

When Sol-o-mon had been king for four years, he laid out the plan that Da-vid had made for the house of the Lord.

He had a talk with Hi-ram the king of Tyre, and told him that it was time to build the house. And the King of Tyre was glad, and did all he could to aid him. He sent So-lo-mon great trees from the woods, and sent him men to help in the work; men who had skill with the ax, and with fine tools of all sorts.

The house was built of stone, and each stone was hewn from the rock, cut so as to fit in the wall ere it was brought to the place where it was to stand, so that no ax nor tools should be used in the house when it was put up.

The walls of the rooms were in-laid with gold, and gems, and the floor of the place where the ark was kept was of pure gold, and in front of the shrine were loops and chains of fine gold.

The doors of the house were made of the wood of the fir tree, and they were carved with great skill, and touched up with gold.

It took Sol-o-mon sev-en years to build the house of the Lord; and when it was done he made a feast, and the priests brought the ark of the Lord from Mount Zi-on where Da-vid kept it.

And all the tribes of Is-ra-el came to Je-ru-sa-lem, that they might be there when the ark was brought.

And when the ark was put in its place, and the priests came out, there was such a cloud in the house that all stood still. For the Lord was in the cloud.

Then Sol-o-mon stood up, and with raised hands asked him to come down and dwell in the house, and to dwell in men's hearts, that they might walk in the right way, and love God all their days.

**QUEEN OF SHE-BA.**

Now the fame of Sol-o-mon came to the ears of a rich queen, who dwelt at She-ba, and she thought she would like to see if this man was as wise and rich as he was said to be. She had a long way to come, and a great train came with her, and these brought loads of rich spice, and gold and sil-ver and gems of worth. And the queen had a talk with Sol-o-mon and he told her all she ought to know.

And she said to the king, What I had heard of thee in my own lands I did not think could be true. So I came to see for my-self, and I find the half was not told to me. So she gave rich gifts to Sol-o-mon, and he gave rich gifts to her, and the queen went back to her own land.

Now it was thought no sin in those days for a man to have more than one wife. And some of Sol-o-mon's wives had been brought up to serve false gods. And it was a sin for the king to wed with such. And as he grew old these wives made him serve their Gods, and turn from the true God whom he had been taught to love and fear.

And this did not please to Lord, and he said that Sol-o-mon's son should not be king when Sol-o-mon died. For Da-vid's sake he would let him be a prince of two tribes all the days of his life. But ten tribes he would take from him.

And foes rose up to plague Sol-o-mon, and for his sins he had to give up the peace and rest that had long been his. When he had been king for two-score years Sol-o-mon died, and his fame has come down to this day, for no man has been born in-to the world so wise and great as King Sol-o-mon.

# CHAPTER XVI.

## ELIJAH.

A-HAB was the last of the six kings who ruled the ten tribes. And he made them serve Ba-al, and built a house for this false god.

These acts did not please God, so he sent E-li-jah, a seer, to tell A-hab that for years and years there should be no rain in the land. And he told E-li-jah to hide near a brook from which he should drink, and the birds of the air would bring him food to eat.

E-li-jah did as the Lord told him, and he drank from the brook, and the birds brought him his food from day to day. But as there was no rain, the brook dried up, and there was lack of food in the land.

So the Lord told E-li-jah to go to the town of Za-re-phath, where a wo-man dwelt who would give him food.

And when E-li-jah came to the gate of the town, a poor wo-man drew near him to pick up some sticks. And he said to her, Bring me a drink, I pray thee.

And as she went, he said, Bring me, I pray thee, a bit of bread in thine hand.

**E-LI-JAH FED BY RA-VENS.**

And she said, As the Lord lives, I have no bread in the house, and but a handful of meal, and a few drops of oil. And I came out to pick up a few sticks that I might light the fire, and bake a small loaf for me and my son, that we may eat it and die.

**E-LI-JAH AND THE WID-OW's CHILD.**

E-li-jah said, Fear not; go and do as thou hast said. But first make me a small loaf, and then make one for thee and thy son. For thus saith the Lord, The meal shall not waste, nor the cruse of oil fail till the day the Lord sends rain on the earth.

So the wo-man went her way and did as E-li-jah told her, and there was from that time no lack of food in her house. But one day her son was ill, and he grew worse and worse, and then died.

When E-li-jah heard of it, he said, Give me thy son. And he took the child from her arms and bore him to his own room, and laid him on his bed.

And E-li-jah cried to the Lord, and said, O Lord, I pray thee let this child's soul come back to him.

And the Lord sent back the soul of the child, and E-li-jah took the boy and brought him to his moth-er.

And she said to E-li-jah, Now by this I know that thou art a man of God, and that the word of the Lord in thy mouth is truth.

For three years there had been no rain in the land, and at the end of that time the Lord said to E-li-jah, Go show thy-self to A-hab, and I will send rain on the land.

So E-li-jah went, and on the way he met with one of A-hab's head men, who loved the Lord. He knew E-li-jah, and bade him turn back, for the king would be sure to put him to death. But E-li-jah said that he would show him-self to A-hab that day. So the man told the king that E-li-jah was near, and the king came out to meet him.

And he found fault with E-li-jah, for he thought he was to blame for the lack of food, and for the long drouth.

E-li-jah told the king to have all those he ruled meet in a mass at one place. And when they came there, E-li-jah cried out to them, How long will ye turn your hearts from God?

And he told them to prove which was the true God, Ba-al or E-li-jah's God. And he told them to bring two young bulls, and to take the flesh of one and lay it on the wood in front of Ba-al, and he would lay the flesh of the oth-er young bull on the Lord's al-tar. And he said, Call ye on your gods and I will call on mine, and let the God that sends down fire be the God whom we all shall serve.

And they said it was a good plan.

So they cried out from sun-rise till noon, O Ba-al hear us! But there was no voice or sign that their god heard them.

E-li-jah said, Cry with a loud voice for he is a god. He may be a-sleep, or lost in thought.

## THE LIT-TLE CLOUD.

And they cried, and made a great noise, and at last fought with their knives till they drew blood.

And E-li-jah said, Come near me.

And they all came near to him.

And E-li-jah took twelve stones, and built an al-tar to the Lord. And he put the flesh and the wood on it, and the wood was wet through and through.

Then he cried out, Hear me, O Lord, hear me, and let it be known that thou art the true God.

Then fire came down from on high and burnt up the flesh, and the wood and the stones, and the dust; and the ground that had been made so wet was as dry as it could be.

And when the crowd saw this they all bowed down to the ground, and said, The Lord he is God! The Lord he is God!

And they broke up the false gods, and gave their hearts for a while to the Lord.

Then E-li-jah told A-hab that he might eat and drink, for the rain would soon set in. And he went to the top of a high mount to pray for rain. Not a cloud was in the sky. The sea was calm. But E-li-jah knew that he must watch, and wait, and pray, and the sign would come.

At last there rose up out of the sea—that is, where the sea and sky seem to meet—a small cloud, the size of a man's hand. And soon the sky was black with clouds, and the wind blew, and there was a great storm of rain.

Now A-hab had a bad wife, and when he told her what E-li-jah had done, she made a vow to kill him.

And E-li-jah had to flee for his life. He was so worn out that when he came to a lone place he sat down in the shade of a tree and wished that he might die. While he slept, an an-gel drew near, at whose touch E-li-jah woke. And the an-gel said, Rise and eat.

**E-LI-JAH AND KING A-HAB.**

And E-li-jah found food and drink set out for him. And he ate and drank, and then lay down and slept. And the an-gel came once more, and bade E-li-jah eat, that he might have strength to go on his way. And he sat up, and ate the food the Lord had sent, and it gave him such strength that he went with-out food for more than a month. And at the end of that time he came to Mount Ho-reb. And he went to a cave and lay down and slept there.

And the Lord spoke to him, and said, Why art thou here, E-li-jah? And E-li-jah said the chil-dren of Is-ra-el had not kept their word, but had gone back to their false gods, and slain all those who sought to turn them from their sins. And I have fled from them, said E-li-jah, for they seek my life.

**E-LI-JAH IN THE WIL-DER-NESS.**

The Lord said, Go forth, and stand on the mount. And there came a great wind that split the high hills, and broke up the rocks. But the Lord was not in the wind.

Then the earth shook, so that there was no firm ground on which to walk; and smoke came up out of the great cracks that were made. But the Lord was not in the earth-quake.

Then there came a still, small voice. When E-li-jah heard it he hid his face in his cloak, and went out and stood at the door of the cave.

And the voice said, Why art thou here, E-li-jah? And El-li-jah said that he fled from those who sought to kill him. And the Lord told him to leave the cave, and go back and pour oil on the head of E-li-sha, who was to take his place.

And E-li-jah found E-li-sha at work with the plough in a large field. And as he went by him he threw his cloak round E-li-sha.

And E-li-sha knew that this meant he must leave all and go with E-li-jah. And he went home to bid fare-well to his dear ones there, and then came back to be near E-li-jah and to wait on him.

**E-LI-JAH GOES TO HEAV-EN.**

Now the time drew near when E-li-jah was to leave the earth. And he and E-li-sha stood near the shore of the Jor-dan. And E-li-jah took his cloak and struck the waves, and they made a wall on each side, and the two men went through on dry land. And as they stood on the oth-er side, E-li-jah said to E-li-sha, Ask what I shall do for thee, ere I leave thee.

And E-li-sha said, Let me, I pray thee, be twice as good and wise as thou.

E-li-jah said, Thou dost ask a hard thing. But if thou dost see me when the Lord takes me from thee, then it shall be so. But if thou dost not see, then it shall not be so.

So they went on, and while they yet spoke, there came a great light in the sky, and the clouds took on strange forms. And E-li-jah was caught up as if by a whirl-wind, and E-li-sha cried out as he saw him pass through the sky, but he was soon out of sight, and E-li-sha saw him no more.

# CHAPTER XVII.

## ELISHA.

**THE CHIL-DREN OF BETH-EL.**

AS E-li-jah rose from the earth he let his cloak fall on E-li-sha. And E-li-sha went down to the Jor-dan, and took the cloak and struck the waves, and they stood up on each side, so that he went a-cross dry shod. And it was made known to all the seers and wise men that E-li-sha had been called to fill E-li-jah's place, and he gave proof that the Lord was with him.

As E-li-sha went from Jer-i-cho to Beth-el, some young folks ran out and made fun of him, and cried, Go up, thou bald head! Go up, thou bald head!

E-li-sha turned back, and asked the Lord to take them in hand. So the Lord sent two great bears out of the wood, and they fell on the chil-dren and tore o-ver two-score of them.

One day E-li-sha came to Shu-nem, where a rich wo-man dwelt. And she bade him come in and eat. And as oft as he went that way, he made it a rule to stop and take the food and drink she set out for him.

And she had a room built for him on the side of her house, and put a bed and a chair in it, that he might go in and out as he chose, and have a place to rest in.

And one day when he was in this room, he sent for the wo-man to come to him. And he said to her, What can I do to pay thee for all thy kind care of us? Shall I speak to the king for thee? She said there was no need, that she sought no pay, and then left the room.

E-li-sha said to his man, What is there that I can do for her?

And the man said, She has no child.

And E-li-sha said, Call her. And she came back and stood at the door. And when the man of God told her that she should have a son, she thought he did not speak the truth.

And the word of the Lord came true, for in less than a year she had a son.

And the child grew up, and went out one day to the field to see the men reap the corn. And while he was there he felt sick, and cried out to his fath-er, My head! my head!

And his fath-er said to a lad, Take the boy home to his moth-er. And she took him, and he sat in her lap till noon, and then died. And she took the boy to E-li-sha's room, and laid him on the bed of the man of God, and then went out and shut the door.

Then she sent for one of the young men, and had him bring an ass to the door, and she got on the ass, and bade the man drive as fast as he could till she told him to stop.

She went till she came near Mount Car-mel. And E-li-sha saw her, and sent Ge-ha-zi out to meet her, and to ask her if it was well with her and with the child. And she said to him, It is well.

But when she came to E-li-sha she fell at his feet, and Ge-ha-zi drew near to push her from the man of God.

But E-li-sha said, Touch her not. She is in great grief, and the Lord has hid it from me and not told me of it.

And the wo-man said, Did I ask thee for a son? Then he knew that the boy was dead.

Then E-li-sha said to Ge-ha-zi, Take my staff, and go thy way with all speed. Stop to speak to no one. And lay my staff on the face of the child.

And the moth-er of the child said, As the Lord lives, I will not leave thee. And E-li-sha rose and went with her, while Ge-ha-zi ran on a-head. And he laid the staff on the face of the child, but the child did not speak nor hear. And he ran out to meet E-li-sha and to tell him the lad did not wake.

And when E-li-sha came to the house he found the child dead, and laid on his bed. So he went in the room and shut the door, and prayed to the Lord.

Then he got on the bed, and lay on the child till his flesh grew warm. Then he left the room for a-while to walk up and down, and when he went back he lay on the child till its breath came back, and it gave signs of life.

And he sent for the moth-er. And when she came to the room he said, Take up thy son. And she fell at the feet of E-li-sha, with thanks too deep for words, and then took her son in her arms and went out.

There was a man in Sy-ri-a, who took charge of all the troops that went to war with the king. This man's name was Na-a-man, and he had done brave deeds, for which he held high rank, and was much thought of. But this man fell ill, and none but those of his own house would go near him. And there was no cure for him. But his wife had a maid to wait on her. And this maid said that if Na-a-man would go to E-li-sha she was sure that he would cure him.

And Na-a-man came down to Sa-ma-ri-a with a note from his own king to the king of Is-ra-el. When the king of Is-ra-el read the note he was ve-ry wroth, and said, Am I God that I can bring the dead to life? For he thought that it was but a trick to bring on a war.

## E-LI-SHA AND THE CHILD.

When E-li-sha heard that the king rent his clothes, he sent word to have Na-a-man come to him.

And Na-a-man drove up in fine style, and stood at the door of E-li-sha's house. And E-li-sha sent word to him to bathe at the Jor-dan sev-en times, and he would be made well.

This put Na-a-man in a rage, for he thought that E-li-sha would come out to him and call on the name of God, and touch him so as to heal him.

And he said, Are there not streams in Da-mas-cus in which I can bathe and be made well? And he went off in a rage.

But some of his men drew near, and said, My lord, if he had bid thee do some great thing wouldst thou not have done it? Why not then do as he says, and wash and be clean?

And Na-a-man gave heed to their words and went down to the Jor-dan. And he took sev-en baths, and then his flesh grew as soft and pink as the flesh of a child, and health and strength came back to him. And Na-a-man went back to E-li-sha's house, he and all his men, and he said, Now I know there is no God in all the earth but the God of Is-ra-el.

Now the time drew near when E-li-sha was to die. And the king, Jo-ash, came to see him as he lay sick in bed.

And E-li-sha said, Take the bow and the darts. And the king took them. And E-li-sha said, Put thy hands on the bow. And the king did so, and E-li-sha put his hands on the king's hands. Then E-li-sha said, Throw wide the east win-dow. And when this was done he said shoot. And the king shot; and E-li-sha told him that he should set Is-ra-el free from its foes.

Then he said to the king, Take the darts. And he took them. And E-li-sha said, Strike them on the ground. And the king struck them on the ground three times, and no more.

**THE AR-ROW OF DE-LIV-ER-ANCE.**

And the man of God was wroth with him, and said, Thou shouldst have struck five or six times, for then thou wouldst have laid the Sy-ri-ans low, now thou shalt smite them but three times.

And E-li-sha died, and was laid in the ground. And one day as some of the folks went out with a dead man to lay him in the grave that was dug for him, they saw a band of thieves from the land of Mo-ab and did not dare to go on. So they put the dead man in the grave where E-li-sha lay. And as soon as the corpse touched the bones of E-li-sha the man came to life and stood on his feet.

# CHAPTER XVIII.

## JONAH, THE MAN WHO TRIED TO HIDE FROM GOD.

THERE was a seer in Is-ra-el whose name was Jo-nah. And the Lord told Jo-nah to go to Nin-e-veh, a large town where there was great need of good men. But Jo-nah did not care to go there, so he ran down to Jop-pa and found a ship there that would set sail for Tar-shish in a few days. So he paid his fare, and went on board the ship to go to Tar-shish, where he seemed to think the Lord would not find him.

But as soon as the ship was well on its way, the Lord sent forth a great wind, and the waves rose high, and the storm beat the ship, and it was blown here and there as if it were a toy. And those on board of her were in great fear, and cried out to their gods, and threw all the goods that were in the ship in-to the sea, so that she would not sink.

Jo-nah was down in the hold, where he lay and slept, though the storm was so fierce.

And the one who had charge of the ship came to him and said, What does this mean? Rise, and call on thy God to save us from ship-wreck.

**JO-NAH IN THE STORM.**

And the rest of the men said, Come, and let us cast lots that we may know who is to blame for this.

So they cast lots, and the lot fell on Jo-nah. And they said to him, Tell us, we pray thee, who has brought on us these ills. What is thy trade? where dost thou come from? where dost thou live? and of what tribe art thou?

And he said I am a Jew, and have fled from the Lord who made the sea and sky.

And the men were in great fear and said, Why hast thou done this thing? And what shall we do to thee that the sea may be still for us? For the waves were rough, and the winds blew a gale.

And Jo-nah said to the men, Take me up and cast me in-to the sea; then shall the sea be calm for you, for I know it is for my sake that this great storm has come up-on you.

The men did not want to drown Jo-nah, so they tried their best to bring the ship to land, but could not.

Then they cried to the Lord, O Lord, we pray thee, count it no sin to us that we take this man's life, for thou, O Lord, hast sent this storm on us for some of his sins.

So they took up Jo-nah, and cast him in-to the sea, and the sea grew still and calm.

And when the men saw this they were in great fear, and brought gifts to the Lord, and made vows that they would serve him.

Now the Lord had sent a great fish to the side of the ship to take Jo-nah in-to its mouth as soon as he was thrown in-to the sea.

And Jo-nah was in-side the fish for three days and three nights. And he prayed to the Lord while he was in the fish; and cried to God to help him, and to blot out his sins. And God heard him, and bade the fish throw him up on the dry land.

Then the Lord spoke to Jo-nah once more, and said, Rise, and go to Nin-e-veh, and preach to it as I bid thee.

And Jo-nah rose and went.

And when God saw them turn from their sins and pray to him, he did not do to Nin-e-veh as he said he would.

But this did not please Jo-nah. He thought that Nin-e-veh should be brought low, for those who dwelt there were not good friends to the Jews. Then, too, Jo-nah's pride was hurt, for he knew that men would laugh at him, and have no faith in what he said, so he went out of the town and sat down by the road-side.

And God made a vine to grow up there in one night, that Jo-nah might sit in its shade and find rest from his grief. And Jo-nah was glad when he saw the gourd. The next morn God sent a worm to gnaw the root of the vine, and it soon dried up.

When the sun rose God sent a hot wind, and the sun beat on Jo-nah's head so that he grew sick and fell in a faint. And he was wroth, and had no wish to live.

And God said to Jo-nah, Is it well for thee to be in such grief for the loss of a gourd?

And Jo-nah said, Yes. There was good cause why he should feel as he did and long to die.

Then the Lord said to him, Thou wouldst have had me spare this vine which cost thee nought, and which grew up in a night and died in a night. And why should I not spare Nin-e-veh—that great town—in which are hosts and hosts of young folks who do not know their right hand from their left?

So God put Jo-nah to shame, and made him see what a sin it was to wish to crush Nin-e-veh just to please his own self and for fear men would laugh at him.

And Jo-nah found out, what we all need to learn, that it is of no use to try to hide from God.

# CHAPTER XIX.

## DANIEL.

THERE was a king of Bab-y-lon whose name was Neb-u-chad-nez-zar. And he sent one of his chief men to choose some of the young Jews who had been well brought up, that they might wait on him.

The chief chose four youths whose name were Dan-i-el, Sha-drach, Me-shach and A-bed-ne-go. And these were brought to Bab-y-lon, that they might be taught as the king wished.

And the Lord was with these four young men, and made them wise, and strong in mind, and fair of face.

**KING NEB-U-CHAD-NEZ-ZAR.**

When they had been taught for three years they were brought to the king's house. And the king kept them near him, and made use of them, for he found that they knew ten times more than all the wise men in the whole realm.

One night the king had a dream that woke him out of his sleep. And he sent for all the wise men—those who could read stars, and those who could work charms—to tell what the dream meant.

And they all came, but none of them could tell the dream that had gone out of the king's own head. And no king, they said, would ask such a thing of wise men.

The king was wroth at this and gave word that all the wise men should be put to death. And they sought Dan-i-el and his friends, that they might kill them.

Dan-i-el said, Why is there such haste? And when he was told he went in to the king and said if he would give him time he would make his dream clear to him.

In the night God showed the king's dream to Dan-i-el, and all that it meant was made clear to him. And Dan-i-el gave praise and thanks to God who had been so good to him.

Then he went to the chief, and told him not to slay the wise men, but to bring him in to the king.

Then Dan-i-el told the king his dream, and all that would come to pass, and when the king heard it he fell on his face be-fore Dan-i-el and said to him, It is true that your God is a God of gods, and a Lord of kings, and that nought is hid from him, since thou hast told me this dream.

And the king made Dan-i-el a great man, and gave him rich gifts, and put him at the head of all the wise men in the land.

Now king Neb-u-chad-nez-zar made a great god out of gold, and set it on one of the plains of Bab-y-lon.

**NEB-U-CHAD-NEZ-ZAR'S DREAM.**

And one of the king's men cried out with a loud voice, and said it was the king's law that all should bow down to the god of gold that he had set up. And those who did not bow down were to be thrown in-to a great hot fire and burnt up.

And some men brought word to the king that the three Jews would not serve his gods, or bow down to this one of gold which he had set up.

These three men were brought to the king, and he said to them, Is it true, O Sha-drach, Me-shach, and A-bed-ne-go that ye will not serve my gods or bow down to the one of gold which I have set up? And he said he would give them one more chance, and if they did not bow down when they heard the call, they should be cast in the same hour in-to the flames. The three Jews said to the king, Be it known to thee now that we will not serve thy gods, nor bow down to the new one thou hast set up. And if we are cast in the fire, the God whom we serve will save us from death and bring us out of thy hands, O king.

Then was the king in a great rage, and he sent word that a fierce fire should be made. And the three Jews were bound and thrown in-to the flames with all their clothes on. And the fire was so hot and they went so near that sparks flew out and killed the men who took up Sha-drach, Me-shach and A-bed-ne-go.

These three Jews fell down in the midst of the flames, but soon rose to their feet, and the Lord would not let the flames burn them.

When the king saw this he rose in great haste and said to his chiefs, Did we not cast three men bound in the midst of the fire?

And they said, True, O king.

And the king said, Lo, I see four men loose, and they walk through the flames and are not hurt, and the form of the fourth is like to the son of God.

Then the king came to the door of the cage of fire and said to Sha-drach, Me-shach and A-bed-ne-go, Ye who serve the most high God, come forth, and come here.

**DWELL-ING WITH THE BEASTS.**

And the three young Jews came forth out of the midst of the fire, and not a hair of their head was singed, nor were their clothes harmed, nor was the smell of fire on them.

And the king praised the God who had shown that he would save from death those who put their trust in him. And the king made it a law that those who spoke ill of the God of Sha-drach, Me-shach, and A-bed-ne-go should be put to death, and their homes torn down, for there was no God who could save as he could.


For a while the king served God and gave him praise for all he had done for him. But men who thought to please the king, spoke of his great wealth and praised all that he did, so that he grew vain and proud, and thought more of him-self than he did of God.

And the king had a dream that made him shake with fear, and he sent for Dan-i-el. And Dan-i-el feared to tell the king the truth. But the king told him to speak out. Then Dan-i-el told him what would take place.

And it all came on king Neb-u-chad-nez-zar. In the same hour his mind left him and he was not fit to reign. So he was thrust out of doors, and did eat grass with the beasts of the fields. And he lay on the ground, and was wet with the dews, and his hair grew so long that his flesh could not be seen, and his nails were like bird's claws.

And at the end of the sev-en years Neb-u-chad-nez-zar raised his eyes to God, and his mind came back to him, and he spoke in praise of the most High.

And Neb-u-chad-nez-zar was made king once more, and grew strong and great, and gave the praise to God; the King of kings, who could raise up those who were down, and bring down those who were full of pride.

When Neb-u-chad-nez-zar died, a new king was on the throne of Bab-y-lon whose name was Bel-shaz-zar. And Bel-shaz-zar made a great feast, and much wine was drunk. And the king sent for the rich cups which his fath-er had brought from the Lord's house in Je-ru-sa-lem. And he and all at the feast drank from these cups, which was a great sin.

In the midst of the feast there came forth a man's hand, that wrote on the wall of the king's house.

And the king saw the hand, and was in great fear, and sent at once for all his wise men.

**THE WRIT-ING ON THE WALL.**

But none of them could read what was on the wall, and the king knew not what to do. Then Dan-i-el was sent for, and the king said he should have great wealth and high rank if he could read the words on the wall.

Dan-i-el said, Keep thy gifts, O king, and give thy fees to some one else. Yet will I read the words on the wall and tell you what they mean. For the God who gives thee life and takes care of thee, thou hast no word of praise. And so God sent this hand to write on the wall.

ME-NE, ME-NE, TE-KEL, U-PHAR-SIN,

which means that thy reign as king is at an end.

When Dan-i-el had told what the hand wrote on the wall, and what the words meant, Bel-shaz-zar bade his men clothe him in red, and put a gold chain on his neck, and make it known that he was to be third in rank from the king.

**DAN-I-EL IN THE LIONS' DEN.**

That same night Bel-shaz-zar was slain, and Da-ri-us took his place on the throne.

Now Da-ri-us was pleased with Dan-i-el, and thought him such a wise and good man that he made him chief of a large force of men who held high rank. And this made these men hate Dan-i-el, and they tried to find out some ill that he had done that they might tell it to the king. But they could find no fault in him. Then they thought of a way in which they could harm him.

They came to the king and asked him to make a law that if one should ask help of God or man for one month, he should be cast in-to a den of li-ons.

They might ask help of the king, but of no one else.

And the king told them to write down this law, and he put his name to it.

When Dan-i-el heard of the law which the king had sent out he went to his home and knelt down three times a day with his face to Je-ru-sa-lem, and gave thanks to God first as he had done all his life.

And the men who were on the watch to catch him in some crime, drew near his house and heard him pray to his God. So they went and told the king, and the king was wroth to think he had made such a law. And he tried his best to save Dan-i-el. But the men held him to his word, and said it would not do for him to change a law that had been made.

**ROCK GRAVE OF DA-RI-US.**

Then the king bade them bring Dan-i-el and cast him in the den of wild beasts. And he said to Dan-i-el, Thy God, whom thou dost serve so well, will be sure to save thee.

And a stone was brought and laid on the mouth of the den.

Then the king went to his own house, but would take no food, nor did he sleep all that night. And at dawn he rose and went in haste to the den of wild beasts. And as he drew near he cried out with a sad voice, O Dan-i-el, canst thy God save thee from the li-ons?

And Dan-i-el said, O king, my God hath shut the li-ons' mouths so that they have not hurt me, since I had done no wrong in his sight nor in thine, O king.

**CY-RUS, KING OF PER-SI-A.**

Then the king was glad, and bade his men take Dan-i-el out of the den. And when he was brought out, there was not a scratch found on him, for his trust was in God, and God took care of him.

Then the king had those men who found fault with Dan-i-el, thrown in-to the den—they and their wives, and their chil-dren—and the wild beasts were quick to eat them up.

Then Da-ri-us made a law that all men should serve the God of Dan-i-el, who was the one true God.

When Da-ri-us died, Cy-rus was made king.

# CHAPTER XX.

## THE GOOD QUEEN ESTHER.

FAR back in the past, wise men had fore-told that the Jews would be kept out of Je-ru-sa-lem for three-score and ten years, and at the end of that time a king, Cy-rus, would let them go back to the land they came from. And he did so.

Not all the Jews went back to their own land, but some of them made their homes in Per-si-a and else-where. And King A-has-u-e-rus was on the throne.

In the third year of his reign he made a great feast.

And he sent for Vash-ti, the queen, to throw off her veil and let his guests see how fair she was.

But Vash-ti would not do it.

Then the king was in a rage, and said to his wise men, What shall we do to Queen Vash-ti to make her know that the king's will is her law?

And the wise men said, Vash-ti hath done wrong to the king and to all the lords of the land.

For when this is told, wives will not do as their liege lords wish. They will say, The king sent word for Vash-ti, the queen, to be brought to him, but she came not. Let the king make a law and put Vash-ti from him and choose a new queen, that all wives, great and small, may take heed and do as they are told.

The king and all the lords thought these were wise words. And the king made it a law that a man should rule in his own house.

Then some of the king's men, whose place it was to wait on him, came to him and said it would be a good plan for him to have all the fair maids in the land brought to his house, that he might choose one of them to be queen, in the place of Vash-ti.

And the king did as they said.

Now there was a Jew in the king's house, whose name was Mor-de-ca-i. He was a poor man, and was there to wait on the king.

And there was a maid named Es-ther, who was one of his kins-folk. And she was "fair of face, and full of grace."

And when the word went forth from the king, scores and scores of fair young maids came to the king's house, and Es-ther came with them. And one of the king's men had them all in his charge.

This man was so pleased with Es-ther that he was more kind to her than he was to the rest, and sent maids to wait on her, and put her and her maids in the best part of the house where the wo-men were. But Es-ther had not let it be known that her folks were Jews, for Mor-de-ca-i had told her not to tell it.

**ES-THER AND THE KING.**

As soon as the king saw Es-ther he fell in love with her, and set the crown on her head, and made her queen in the place of Vash-ti.

Then the king made a great feast, and gave gifts to the poor for the new queen's sake. And she had not yet made it known that her folks were Jews.

Now two of the king's men, who stood on guard at the doors of his house, were wroth with the king and sought to kill him.

And their plot was known to Mor-de-ca-i, who was a watch-man at the king's gate. And he told it to Es-ther, and she told it to the king, and both of the men were hung. And what Mor-de-ca-i had done to save the king's life was put down in a book.

And in this same book was set down all that took place in the king's reign.

Now there was in the king's house a man whose name was Ha-man. And the king gave him a high place, and bade those of low rank bow down to Ha-man.

But the Jew at the gate would not bow when Ha-man went in and out. And the rest of the men who stood by told Ha-man of it.

Now Ha-man was a vain man, and when he saw that Mor-de-ca-i did not bow to him as the rest did he was full of wrath. It had been made known to him that Mor-de-ca-i was a Jew.

And so he told the king if he would make a law that all the Jews should be put to death, he would give him a large sum of gold and sil-ver.

The king heard what Ha-man said, and then took his ring from his hand and gave it to Ha-man, and told him to do with the Jews as he thought best. The king gave him his ring that he might use it as a seal. And Ha-man set the scribes to work, and they wrote just what he told them, in the king's name. And when the wax was put at the end with the king's seal on it, it was the same as if the whole had been writ by the king's own hand.

Men were sent out in haste to make the law known through-out the land, that all the Jews in Per-si-a were to be slain. And when this was done Ha-man and the king sat down to drink wine.

When Mor-de-ca-i heard of the law that Ha-man had made, he rent his clothes and put on sack-cloth, and went out and cried with a loud cry. And he came and stood in front of the king's gate, though he could not pass through, for it was the law that none should pass who wore sack-cloth. And all through the land the Jews were in deep grief, so full of tears that they could eat no food; and not a few of them put on sack-cloth to show the depth of their woe.

Queen Es-ther had not heard of the law, but her maids came and told her of the state Mor-de-ca-i was in. And her grief was great, and she sent food and clothes to him, and bade the men take the sack-cloth from him. But Mor-de-ca-i would take nought from their hands, nor change his clothes.

Then the queen sent one of her head men, Ha-tach, to ask Mor-de-ca-i what was the cause of his grief, and why he had put on sack-cloth.

And Mor-de-ca-i told Ha-tach of the law that had been made, and what a large sum Ha-man had said he would give to the king if he would kill off all the Jews in the land.

And he told Ha-tach to tell the queen, and to show her what the scribes wrote, and bid her see the king and ask him to save the Jews.

And Ha-tach took the word to the queen.

Es-ther bade him tell her kins-man that it was well known that those who went in to the king when they had not been sent for, would be put to death. But if the king held out his gold wand it was a sign that he would spare their lives. The king has not sent for me for a month, said she. How then can I go to him?

Mor-de-ca-i sent back word to the queen to think not that the king would spare her life if the Jews were put to death. And it might be that God had put her in the place she held that she might keep the Jews at this time.

Then Es-ther sent word to him that he and all the Jews in the king's court should fast and pray for her, and not eat or drink for three days and three nights.

I and my maids will do the same, said the queen, and I will go in to the king in spite of the law; and if I die, I die in a good cause.

So on the third day af-ter the queen put on her rich robes, and went in and stood ve-ry near to the throne on which the king sat.

**ES-THER AT SHUS-HAN.**

And when the king saw her, God put it in-to his heart to be kind, and he held out to her the gold wand that was in his hand. And the queen drew near, and touched the tip of the wand.

Then the king said, What wilt thou, Queen Es-ther? and what wouldst thou ask of me? Were it half of my realm I would give it to thee.

The queen said, If it please the king, I would like him and Ha-man to come this day to a feast I have made for them.

And the king bade Ha-man make haste, and they both went to the feast. And while they drank the wine the king told the queen to make known her wish.

But she put him off and said she would tell him the next day, if he and Ha-man would come to the feast that she would spread for them.

And Ha-man's heart was full of pride, since the queen chose him and no one else to feast with her and the king. And when he went out he felt that all men ought to bow down to him. But Mor-de-ca-i would not. And Ha-man told all his friends how kind the king and queen were to him, and what high rank he held, and said that his life would be full of joy if it were not for the Jew at the king's gate.

Ha-man's wife told him to fix a rope to a tall tree, and speak to the king the next day and have him hang the Jew. And Ha-man made a slip-noose at the end of a rope, and had the rope made fast to a tall tree.

Now that night the king could not sleep. And he sent for the book in which was put down all that took place in the realm, and had it read to him. And when he who read came to the part which told what Mor-de-ca-i had done to save the king's life, the king said, How has Mor-de-ca-i been paid for this deed?

And the man said he had had nought, and still kept watch at the king's gate.

Then the king heard a step and sent one of his men to see who it was.

Now Ha-man had come to the king's house to ask him to hang Mor-de-ca-i. And the man came back and said that Ha-man stood in the court. And the king said, Let him come in.

So Ha-man came in. And the king said to him, What shall be done to the man who has won the praise of the king?

And Ha-man thought, That means me, of course, and no one else.

And he said to the king, Let the robes be brought that the king wears, and the horse he rides, and the crown which is set on his head. And let the robes and the crown be put on the man whom the king has in mind, and bring him on horse-back through the street of the town, and have men cry out, Thus shall it be done to the man who has won the praise of the king.

And the king said to Ha-man, Make haste and take the robes and the horse as thou hast said, and do thus and no less to the Jew at the king's gate.

But Ha-man went home, and was full of shame. And he told his wife and his friends of his hard fate. And while they yet spake the king's men came for him to go to the queen's feast. And while they ate and drank, the king bade the queen make known her wish. Ask what thou wilt; were it half my realm, I would give it to thee.

Then the queen said, If it please thee, O king, take my life and spare the lives of all the Jews. For we have been sold and the truth has not been told of us, and we are to be put to death. The king said, Who is he, and where is he who has dared to do this thing?

And the queen told him it was Ha-man. And Ha-man was in great fear as he stood face to face with the king and queen.

The king rose in great wrath and went out of doors, and when he came in he saw Ha-man at the feet of the queen, where he went to beg her to save his life.

And when the king was shown the rope and the tree on which Ha-man meant to hang Mor-de-ca-i he said, Hang *him* on it. And they hung Ha-man, and the king's wrath left him.

And on the same day the king gave Ha-man's house to Es-ther, and Mor-de-ca-i was brought in to the king, who had been told that he was a kins-man of the queen. And the king gave him the ring which Ha-man had worn, and the queen put him at the head of the house in which Ha-man had dwelt.

But Es-ther was still sad at heart be-cause of the law that had been made, that all the Jews in the land should be put to death. And she went in once more to the king—though he had not sent for her—and fell down at his feet in tears. Then the king held out the wand of gold, and the queen rose, and stood be-fore the king and asked him to change the law and save the lives of the Jews.

The king could not change the law, but he told Es-ther and Mor-de-ca-i to make a law that would please them and sign it with the king's seal. So they made a law that the Jews should kill all those who came to do them harm. And when Mor-de-ca-i came out from his talk with the king he had on a robe of blue and white, such as the king wore, and a gold crown on his head.

And all the Jews were glad; and when the day came that Ha-man had set for the Jews to be slain, the Jews went out and fought for their lives and put their foes to rout. And grief gave place to joy, and a feast was held for two days. This feast was called the Feast of Pu-rim, which the Jews keep to this day.

The Jews who had gone to Je-ru-sa-lem to build up its walls were still at work there. But there were foes to watch, and the poor Jews found fault with the rich ones, and there was strife in their midst from year to year. But when Ne-he-mi-ah went to their aid the Lord gave him strength to set things straight, and in a year the new wall was built and the gate put up. Then there was a great feast, and all the Jews gave praise and thanks to God.

But they went back to their sins, and did not serve God as they ought. And kings fought for Je-ru-sa-lem and took it from their hands and made the Jews their slaves.

And at last the Ro-mans came and took Je-ru-sa-lem and broke down its walls, and made the Jews serve them. And He-rod, who had led the Ro-mans to war, was made their king. He was a fierce, bad man, who would let no one rule but him-self. He put his own wife and two of his sons to death, and did all that he could to make folks hate and fear him.

He tried to make the Jews think that he was one of their race, but he was not. He thought it would please them if he built up their House of God, so he set men to work to tear down the old and to put up the new, and they made use of much gold and sil-ver and fine white stones.

There was no ark to put in it, for that had been lost, but a large stone was put in the place where the ark should have been.

And it took He-rod more than nine years to build this House of God on the top of Mount Mo-ri-ah. And the way up to it was by a long flight of steps.

This ends the Old Tes-ta-ment, which was made up of all the books that were kept by all the scribes from the time the world was made.

# The New Testament

CHRIST IN THE TEM-PLE.

THE BABE OF BETH-LE-HEM.

# HISTORY OF THE NEW TESTAMENT.

## CHAPTER I.

### THE BIRTH OF CHRIST.

THE time was near for Je-sus to come on the earth. God had told Ad-am and Eve of one who would save them from their sins. Mo-ses, and all the seers and wise men, spoke of him who was to give men new hearts, and help them to lead new lives.

In the days of He-rod, king of Ju-dah, there was a priest named Zach-a-ri-as. His wife's name was E-liz-a-beth. They were both old, and had led pure lives, and sought to keep God's laws. But they had no child.

One day when the priest was in the house of God by one of the al-tars, an an-gel came and stood near him. And when the priest saw him he shook with fear.

But the an-gel said: Fear not, Zach-a-ri-as, for God will give thee and thy wife a son, and thou shalt call his name John.

He shall be great in the sight of the Lord, and shall not drink wine nor strong drink, and shall turn the hearts of men to the Lord their God.

Then Zach-a-ri-as said to the an-gel, But how shall I know that these things will be?

And the an-gel said to him, I am the an-gel Ga-bri-el, who stands near to God, and he has sent me to tell thee this good news. And for thy lack of faith thou shalt be dumb, and speak not a word till the day that these things come to pass.

Now those who were in the courts of God's house thought it strange that Zach-a-ri-as should stay so long at the al-tar where he burnt the in-cense.

And when he came out he could not speak to them, but made them know by signs that he had seen a strange sight.

Six months from this time God sent the an-gel Ga-bri-el to the town of Naz-a-reth, to a young wo-man there whose name was Ma-ry. She was one of the heirs of King Da-vid.

When Ma-ry saw the an-gel she was in great fear, for she knew not why he had come. And the an-gel said: Fear not, Ma-ry, for God has blessed thee. Thou shalt have a son, and shalt call his name JE-SUS. He shall be great, and shall be called the Son of God. And God will make him a king, and to his reign there shall be no end.

Ma-ry said: How can this be?

**THE AN-NUN-CIA-TION.**

The an-gel told her that what might seem hard for her was not hard for God, who could do all things. He had told E-liz-a-beth that she should have a son, and he had now sent word to Ma-ry that she should have a son; and what he had said he would do.

Then Ma-ry said, Let the Lord's will be done. And the an-gel left her.

Ma-ry made haste and went to the land of Ju-dah, and to the house of E-liz-a-beth and Zach-a-ri-as, where she spent three months. Then she came back to her own home. Jo-seph was the name of Ma-ry's hus-band; and he was a Jew, of King Da-vid's line. They were both poor, and Jo-seph had to work hard at his trade. He was a car-pen-ter.

God gave Zach-a-ri-as and E-liz-a-beth the son that he said they should have. And when the child was eight days old, the friends and kins-folk came to see it and to give it a name. Most of them said, Call him Zach-a-ri-as.

But the child's mo-ther said, Not so. He shall be called John.

And they said, There is none of thy kin-dred that is called by this name.

And they made signs to the fa-ther that he should let them know by what name the child should be called.

And the fa-ther sat down and wrote: His name is John. And they all thought this strange, as he had not told them of the an-gel who spoke to him in the house of God.

As soon as Zach-a-ri-as wrote these words his speech came back to him, and he gave praise and thanks to God. And all the folks in that part of the land heard of these things, and they said, What sort of a child shall this be? And the boy grew tall and strong, and the Lord blest him, and he went out and dwelt in the woods and waste lands till he was a man, and it was time for him to preach to the Jews and to tell them of Je-sus.

Now the king of Rome was called a Ce-sar, in the speech of that land, and the Jews had to do just as he said, for they were his slaves. And he made a law that the names of all the Jews should be put down in a book, that it might be known what tribe they came from, and what they were worth. Then, too, it would not be a hard task to count them when the Ce-sar wished to know how large a force of them was in this land he had fought for and won.

And each Jew was to go to that part of the land where his fore-fa-thers dwelt, and have his name put down in the book at that place.

So, as Jo-seph and his wife were of the house of Da-vid, they both set out for the town of Beth-le-hem, where Da-vid used to feed his sheep. The way was long, and when they came to the town they found a great crowd of folks there. There was no room for Jo-seph and Ma-ry at the inn, and they knew no one at whose house they could stay.

As they went from place to place in search of a room, they came to a shed in which was a great trough or man-ger full of hay, where the poor folks who came to town fed the beasts on which they rode.

So Jo-seph and Ma-ry made their home in this shed while they had to wait to have their names put down. And while they were there God gave to Ma-ry the son that he said she should have.

And as she had no fine soft clothes to wrap the babe in, she took bands of cloth and put round him, and laid him on the straw in the man-ger.

In those days rich men kept large flocks of sheep and goats, and had men watch them at night for fear that wild beasts would seize and kill them. The men who fed and took care of the sheep were called shep-herds.

One night, as some shep-herds were on the hills where they kept watch of their flocks, the an-gel of the Lord came down to them. And a bright light shone round them so that they were in great fear.

**THE NA-TIV-I-TY.**

And the an-gel said to them, Fear not, for I bring you good news which shall give joy to all the land. For Christ, the Lord, is born for you this day, in the town of Beth-le-hem, and he will save you from your sins. And this is the way ye shall know him: Ye shall find the babe wrapped in bands of cloth and laid in a man-ger.

When the an-gel had said this, there came, like a flash of light, a great host of an-gels who gave praise to God, and sang, Glo-ry be to God on high, and on earth, peace and good-will to men.

When the an-gels had left them the shep-herds said, Let us go at once to Beth-le-hem and see these things of which the an-gel has told us.

And they came with haste, and found Ma-ry and Jo-seph, and the babe that lay in the man-ger where the ox and ass used to feed. And when they had seen the child, they went out and told what the an-gel had said to them. And those who heard were filled with awe, for it was the first time that such a thing had been done in the world. And the strange news spread fast.

Ma-ry told no one of the talk she had had with the an-gel, but thought much of these things, and took the best of care of the new-born babe. It did not seem as if it could be her own child.

When the babe was eight days old, its fa-ther and mo-ther gave it the name of JE-SUS, as the an-gel had bid them. And they gave him to the Lord; that is, they vowed to the priest that they would bring up the child to serve God and to lead a good life. For though he was the son of God he was sent on earth to teach men what they ought to do.

Now there was a man in Je-ru-sa-lem whose name was Sim-e-on. He was a good man, and did what was right, and for years he had been on the watch for one of whom the seers had told, and who was to save men from their sins.

And it was made known to Sim-e-on in a dream that he should not die till he had seen this King of kings and Lord of lords.

**SIM-E-ON IN THE TEM-PLE.**

Sim-e-on was a priest in the house of God, and when Jo-seph and Ma-ry brought in the child Je-sus, he took it up in his arms and blest God, and said: Now, Lord, thy words have come true, and I can die in peace, for I have seen him who is to be the light of the world, and to save men from their sins!

- 155 -

Jo-seph and Ma-ry knew not what to make of this strange speech. And the priest blest them, and gave the child back to his mo-ther, and told her of some of the great things he would do when he grew up to be a man.

And there was one An-na, who kept all the fasts, and served God night and day. She was four-score and four years old, and could fore-tell what was to take place, and her fame was great. And she came in-to the house of God while Sim-e-on yet spoke, and gave thanks to the Lord, and told of him who was to come to save the Jews, and to give them back their rights.

Then Ma-ry and Jo-seph went back to their own home in Naz-a-reth. And the child grew, and was strong, and wise, and God blest him from day to day.

# CHAPTER II.

## THE STAR IN THE EAST.

IN these days God spoke to men by strange signs, and wise ones were all the time on the watch for them. They had read in their old books of a star that was to shine with a bright light, and each night they would raise their eyes to the sky, in hopes that they might see this sign that would bring hope and joy to the whole race of Jews. But years and years had gone by, and the Jews had no land of their own, and were as slaves to the Ce-sar of Rome. And He-rod, their king, was most harsh to them, for he had skill in the use of a sword, but not in the use of kind words, or good deeds.

**THE GUID-ING STAR.**

One night as a wise man lay on the roof of his house, with his gaze fixed on the great broad sky, he gave a start and cry of joy, for there shone a new star of such size that all the rest of the stars grew dim and small. And it was as if the sun had burst through a dark cloud, and brought the dawn some hours too soon, for the whole East was full of light from the long rays of this new star.

And the star seemed to move, and its rays to point all one way. And the wise men who saw it knew that the light had come for which they had looked and prayed so long, and they set out at once with the star to guide them, and they took rich gifts with them. Each night it shone in the sky, and led them on and on till they came to Je-ru-sa-lem. And they said to those they met there, Where is he that is born to be King of the Jews? for we have seen his star in the east, and have come to kneel down at his feet.

When He-rod heard of these things, and that they spoke of Je-sus as King, he was in great fear lest he should lose his throne. So he sent for his chief priests and scribes that they might tell him where Christ should be born. And they read from their old books that it had been fore-told that he should be born in Beth-le-hem.

Then He-rod sent for the wise men, and told them to go to Beth-le-hem, and search for the young child. And when ye find him, said he, bring me back word that I too may fall down at his feet and give him praise.

But this he did not mean to do, for his plan was to put the child to death just as soon as he could find out where it was.

**THE SHEP-HERDS OF BETH-LE-HEM.**

When the king had ceased to speak, the wise men from the east left Je-ru-sa-lem, and went on their way to Beth-le-hem. And the star led them on and on, and was like the face of a friend. And a small, still voice seemed to say to them:—Come!—Come!—Come! And it drew them so that they would have gone to the ends of the earth. When troops are on the march, and through their ranks goes the cry of Halt! then each foot must stand still, and not a man moves from his place.

And when the wise men came to Beth-le-hem, lo, the star that had led them stood still in the sky, right o'er the place where the young child was. And when they went in-to the house they saw the young child, with Ma-ry, his mo-ther, and they fell on their knees and bowed down to him as if he had been a king. And they brought him gifts of great worth, and gold and myrrh and rich gums and spice that can be found on-ly in those lands in the far East.

And God spoke to them in a dream, and told them not to go back to He-rod, so they went home not by the same road they had come.

When He-rod found that the wise men had not done as he bade them, he was in a great rage, and sent men to Beth-le-hem, and slew all the chil-dren there who were two years old or less, for then he was sure that Je-sus would be slain.

**THE WISE MEN BRING-ING PRES-ENTS TO JE-SUS.**

But ere He-rod's men came, God spoke to Jo-seph in a dream, and said, Rise, and take thy wife and thy son, and flee in-to E-gypt, and stay there till I bring thee word; for He-rod will seek the young child to kill him.

So Jo-seph did as the Lord told him, and took his wife and child out of Beth-le-hem by night, and went to dwell in the Land of E-gypt.

**THE FLIGHT IN-TO E-GYPT.**

But when He-rod was dead, God spoke to Jo-seph in a dream, and told him to take his wife and son and go back to the land of Is-ra-el, for the man was dead who sought to kill the young child. And Jo-seph did as the an-gel told him, and he and his wife and child came and dwelt in Naz-a-reth.

# CHAPTER III.

## THE BOYHOOD OF JESUS.

It was in the first month of the year that God brought the Jews out of E-gypt and led them through the Red Sea.

And he made it a law that in the first month of each year they should all meet at one place, and bring the young lambs and calves and the first fruits of the field and give thanks to God in the way they had been taught. And this they were to do all the days of their life. And this feast, which was to last not quite two months, was known as the Feast of the Weeks. There were days they were to fast, and days they were to feast, and they were to call to mind that they were once slaves, and that God had set them free, and with glad hearts praise and bless his great name.

The place where the Jews now met was at Je-ru-sa-lem, and Je-sus was twelve years old when he went up for the first time, with Jo-seph and Ma-ry, to keep the Feast of the Weeks.

There was a great crowd there, and friends to meet and talk with, and it must have been a hard task to keep track of the young folks, who found so much to see and to hear that was new and strange.

When the days of the feast were at an end, Jo-seph and Ma-ry set out for their home in Naz-a-reth.

They had gone out with a band of friends and folks from the same town, and were to come back in the same way. It was not safe for them to go by themselves, for there were waste lands to cross where bands of thieves lay in wait for a chance to rob and to kill those who came their way.

**NAZ-A-RETH.**

Some rode on mules, some on horse-back, and some had to walk all the way. Je-sus was not with Jo-seph and Ma-ry, but they thought he must be with some of the friends or kins-folk. But when at the end of a day's ride he came not near them, they sought for him in the groups of friends and kins-folk, where there were lads of his own age.

**JE-SUS WITH THE DOC-TORS IN THE TEM-PLE.**

And when they found him not, they went back to Je-ru-sa-lem, and sought for him with hearts full of grief, for they knew not what harm might have come to him.

For three days they went from house to house, and through the lanes and streets, but could see no signs of the boy they had lost.

At the end of that time they went in-to the house of God, it may have been to pray that their child might be found, and there a strange sight met their gaze.

Je-sus sat in the midst of the wise men, whose place it was to teach and to preach to those who came up to the feasts, and the old men bent their heads to hear what the young lad had to say. For it was the first time they had met with one so young in years who was so wise in speech, and they felt in their hearts that he must have been taught of God.

When Jo-seph and Ma-ry saw Je-sus they were struck dumb, and could do naught but stare, as if it was a scene in a dream. Then Ma-ry said, My son, why didst thou vex us thus? we have sought for thee with sad hearts.

Je-sus said, Why did ye look for me? Do ye not know that I must do the work that my fa-ther has set me to do?

Jo-seph and Ma-ry did not know what he meant by these words, or that God had sent Je-sus on earth to teach men how to read the word of God a-right, and how to save their souls from death.

Je-sus went back to Naz-a-reth with Jo-seph and Ma-ry, and was a good son to them. And he grew wise and tall, and was blest of God, and won the hearts of all who were near him, for they saw in him much to love.

It was not known that he was the Son of God, and he made friends by his own sweet ways, for he was a poor boy.

Naught was heard or known of Je-sus for some years, and we are led to think that he was taught how to use the axe, and saw, and plane, and to work at the same trade his fa-ther did. This gave him a chance to see how folks lived, and to use his eyes and ears as he went from house to house, so that when he went forth to teach he could tell them of their sins, and show them how vile they were.

And this part of the life of Je-sus—of which not a word is told in the New Test-a-ment—is to teach us to stay in the place where God has put us, and to do our work there in the best way we know how.

Je-sus was at school then, just as boys and girls in these days go to school, and strive to grow wise and to fit them-selves for the work they are to do in the world. And though he was to be a king he did not put on airs, or sit and fold his hands and bid those that were near wait on him and be at his beck and call. No! he was born and brought up with poor folks, to teach us that Je-sus is more at home with the poor than he is with the rich; and to be Christ-like we must seek to please God, to do his will, to put down pride, and keep sin out of our hearts.

# CHAPTER IV.

## JESUS AND JOHN THE BAPTIST.

YOU have been told that John went out in-to the woods and waste lands when quite a young man. He fed on lo-custs and wild hon-ey, and his clothes were made of the skin of the cam-el, with the long rough hair on the out-side.

The time had now come for him to go out in the world to tell of Je-sus, and to bid men give up their sins and walk in the right path.

And he went to a place near the Jor-dan and crowds came there to hear him. And he told them that he had been sent to warn them to flee from the wrath to come. He said they must not think they would be saved be-cause they were sons or heirs of good men who had served God and died in the faith. He told them that each one was to be like a tree, and to stand in his place and bring forth fruit, and serve God in the best way that he could. And each tree, said John, which brings not forth good fruit is cut down and cast in-to the fire. He told them they must be good and kind to each oth-er, and must give food and clothes to those who were in need of such things. They must not tell lies, nor steal, nor be vain and proud, but they must show by the way they lived that they loved God and were glad to do his will.

**JOHN THE BAP-TIST.**

And when those who heard him felt a great hate for sin, and a strong wish to lead good lives, and to be saved from the wrath of God, they spoke to John and he led them down to the Jor-dan and they were bap-tiz-ed in the stream.

Now wa-ter will wash the stains from our clothes, and cleanse our skin, but it will not wash our sins away. To do this we must have Christ in our hearts. Some of those who heard John talk thought that he might be the Christ who was to come, and of whom the proph-ets had fore-told since the days of Mos-es. Some were quite sure of it; but oth-ers shook their heads, for they had made up their minds that he who was to come and rule o-ver them would be dressed like a king, and not in such plain clothes as John wore.

John heard their words, or guessed their thoughts, and he said to these Jews, I in-deed bap-tize you with wa-ter, but he who is to come af-fer me, and who is great-er than I, will bap-tize you with fire.

That meant that Je-sus would be in their hearts like a fire, to burn up all that was bad, as they burnt the chaff that was blown loose from the wheat.

Then Je-sus came from his home in Naz-a-reth to have John bap-tize him in Jor-dan's stream. But John would not. He said there was more need that Je-sus should bap-tize him. He felt that there was need to have his own sins washed a-way, but Je-sus had no sins. So why dost thou come to me? said John.

Je-sus had come on the earth as a man to do God's will, and to teach man-kind how to walk in the right path and keep their hearts free from sin. And he told John, that all these things would be made plain to him some day, and it was right that he should bap-tize him.

So John went with Je-sus in-to the wa-ter, and he bap-tized Je-sus in the wa-ter. And Je-sus was pray-ing to his Fa-ther in heav-en.

And as Je-sus went up out of the wa-ter, lo, there came a great light in the sky, that took the form of a dove, and it came down and seemed to rest on him. And God's voice spoke out of the sky, and said: This is my dear Son, with whom I am well pleased.

Then Je-sus went out in-to the waste lands, and was there with no one near him for more than a month. In all that time he ate no food, but spent the hours in talks with God. At last he felt weak and faint, and left the waste lands to go in search of some-thing to eat.

Now there is a fiend in this world, as we all know, who has a black heart, and can take on all sorts of shapes. He came to Eve in the form of a snake, and to Sam-son with a fair face. He tempts those to do wrong who have set out to do right, and we have to be on our guard all the time, and to watch and pray that we may be kept safe from him.

When this fiend saw Je-sus on his way to give new hearts to men, and to make them good and pure, he thought he would try and put a stop to such work. So he went out to tempt Je-sus, with the same smooth voice in which he spoke to Eve.

And he came to him and said, If thou be the Son of God change those stones in-to bread, so that thou canst eat now that thou hast need of food.

Je-sus knew why Sa-tan had come, and he told him that men should take more pains to do God's will than to get bread to eat. Next Sa-tan took Je-sus to Je-ru-sa-lem, and up to a high place where the house of God was built. And he said to him, If thou be the Son of God, throw thy-self down; for it is said, he shall give his an-gels charge to keep thee in all thy ways. They shall bear thee up in their hands lest thou dash a-gainst a stone.

**THE TEMPT-A-TION.**

Je-sus told him that it was not right to go where it was not safe, just to try if God would keep us from harm.

Then Sa-tan took Je-sus up on a high mount, from whence could be seen all the large towns in the land, and all their great wealth. And he said to him, All these will I give thee for thine own if thou wilt kneel down and wor-ship me.

Je-sus said to him, Go from me, Sa-tan, for it is set down in God's book, Thou shalt wor-ship the Lord thy God, and him a-lone shalt thou serve.

When Sa-tan found that Je-sus paid no heed to his words, he left him, and an-gels came to wait on the Son of God.

In a short time Je-sus went back to the Jor-dan where John was, and when John saw him, he said, Be-hold the Lamb of God!

He spoke of Je-sus as the Lamb of God, for he was to be laid on the cross for the sins of men, as the lamb was in those days laid on the al-tar.

Then Je-sus set out to preach and to turn men from their sins. And he went to Gal-i-lee. And one day as he walked by the sea-shore he saw two men cast their net in-to the sea. Their names were An-drew and Pe-ter. Je-sus said to them, Come with me. And they left their nets at once, that they might be near him and learn of him.

**THE MAR-RIAGE IN CA-NA.**

The next day he saw two men whose names were James and John in a boat with their fa-ther. Their nets had broke, and they were in haste to mend them so that they could take in a large haul of fish. But Je-sus spoke to James and John, and they left the boat at once, and went with him that he might teach them.

The next day Je-sus spoke to Phil-ip and Na-than-i-el, and they left their homes and went with him.

When Je-sus came to the town of Ca-na he found quite a crowd there, for a wed-ding was to take place, and he and his mo-ther had been bid to the feast. There was food to eat and wine to drink, but ere the feast was at an end the wine was all gone. And when Ma-ry knew of it she said to Je-sus, They have no wine. And she bade those who were there to serve the guests to do just as Je-sus told them.

Now there were in the house six large stone jars such as the Jews kept to hold wa-ter. Je-sus said to the men, Fill the jars with wa-ter. And they filled them to the brim. And he said to them, Take some out now and bear it to the chief guest of the feast. And they did so; and the wa-ter was changed in-to wine.

The chief guest did not know what Je-sus had done; but when he had drunk some of the wine he sent for the bride-groom and said to him, As a rule, those who give a feast set out the good wine first, and when the guests have had all they care for they bring out that which is worse. But thou hast kept the good wine till now.

This was the first great sign Je-sus gave of the pow-er he had from on high. And it was proof to those whose hearts were with him that he was the true Son of God.

The time of the Feast of Weeks was at hand, and Je-sus went up to Je-ru-sa-lem to keep it. And in one of the courts were men who had brought their wares to the house of God to sell them to the Jews when they came up to the feast. When Je-sus came to the place where these men were, the sight did not please him. And Je-sus made a scourge, or whip of small cords, and drove them all out, with their flocks and their herds. And he poured their gold and sil-ver on the ground, and said to those who sold doves, Take them a-way; make not the house of God a place to buy and sell in.

**DRIV-ING THE SELL-ERS FROM THE TEM-PLE.**

And while he was at the feast crowds were drawn to him, and had faith in him when they saw what won-ders he could do. Nic-o-de-mus, one of the chief men of the Jews, came to Je-sus in the night, and said to him, We know that God has sent thee to teach us what is right, for no man could do these won-ders if God were not with him.

Je-sus told him that he must have a new heart or he could not be a child of God.

He-rod, who slew the babes of Beth-le-hem, was dead, but his son He-rod ruled in that part of Gal-i-lee, and he was a bad man. He took his broth-er's wife from him and made her his own wife. Her name was He-ro-di-as. When John the Bap-tist told He-rod this was not right, he would have put him to death if he had dared. But he had heard him preach, and knew that he was a good man. Yet to please He-ro-di-as He-rod had seized John, and bound him, and shut him up in jail.

While John was in jail, He-rod, on his birth-day, made a great feast for the lords and chief men of Gal-i-lee. And a young girl, whose name was Sa-lo-me, came and danced in their midst. He-rod was so much pleased with her that he said, Ask of me what thou wilt, and thou shalt have it, though it were half of my realm.

And Sa-lo-me went to He-ro-di-as—who was her mo-ther—and said, What shall I ask?

And He-ro-di-as said to her, Ask the king to cut off the head of John the Bap-tist, and bring it to thee here in a large dish.

Sa-lo-me came back in haste to the king, and said, Give me, in a large dish, the head of John the Bap-tist.

He-rod was grieved, but as he had sworn to give her what she asked for, and those who sat near had heard him, he felt bound to keep his word. So he sent one of his train-band, who cut off John's head in the jail, and brought it in a large dish to Sa-lo-me, and she gave it to her mo-ther.

When the friends of John heard of it they came up and took his dead form and laid it in a tomb, and went and told Je-sus.

# CHAPTER V.

## THE WOMAN AT THE WELL—JESUS BY THE SEA.

ONE day Je-sus and his friends came to the town of Sy-char, near which was a well to which all the folks came to draw wa-ter. It was known as Ja-cob's Well. The sun was hot, and Je-sus, tired with his long walk, sat down by this well to rest, while his friends went to the town to buy food.

A wo-man came from the town to draw wa-ter. She led a life of sin, and had no love for God in her heart. And Je-sus knew this, for he sees all our hearts, and knows all our thoughts, and all that we have done.

And he spoke to the wo-man, and told her of the things she had done that did not please God. And she thought he was a seer, to whom God told things that were not known to most folks. And she said to Je-sus, I know that Christ is to come in-to the world, and when he comes he will tell us all things. Je-sus said to her, I that speak to thee am he.

**THE WO-MAN AT THE WELL.**

Then the wo-man left her jar, and made haste back to the town, and said to her friends there, Come and see a man who told me all the things that ever I did. Is not this the Christ?

And they went out and saw Je-sus, and bade him come in-to the town. And he went with them, and was there for three days. And they gave ear to the things he taught them. And they said to the wo-man, Now we have faith in him, not be-cause of the things thou didst tell us, but be-cause we have heard him our-selves, and know that he is the Christ whom God has sent down to us.

From there he went once more to the town of Ca-na. And a rich man came from the town where he dwelt to ask Je-sus to come and heal his son, who was sick. And the rich man said to him, Come as quick as you can, lest my child should die.

Je-sus said to him, Go thy way, thy son is made well.

The rich man knew that Je-sus would not say what was not true, and with a glad heart went back to his home. And as he drew near the house his slaves ran out to meet him, and said to him, Thy son is well.

The rich man bade them tell him what time the change took place, and they told the hour that the fe-ver left the lad. And it was the same hour that Je-sus had said to the rich man, Thy son is well. And he and all those in his house felt in their hearts that Je-sus was the son of God.

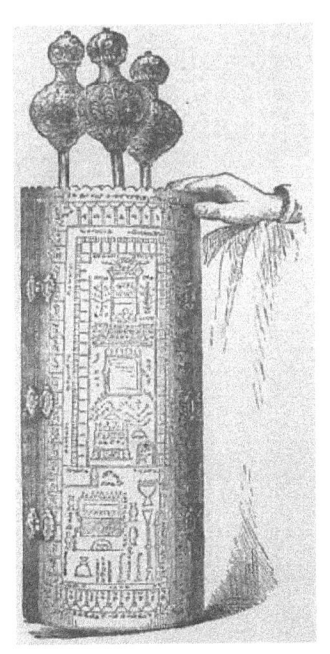

**CYL-IN-DER HOLD-ING THE PENT-A-TEUCH.**

The Jews did not yet know how to print, and they had no books such as we have. They wrote with pen and ink on rolls of parch-ment, made from the skin of sheep and goats.

These rolls were kept in the house of God, in a box or chest called an ark, and were brought out and read to those who came to the church on the Lord's day. The chief rolls, all the books of the Old Tes-ta-ment, were kept at Je-ru-sa-lem, but as all the Jews could not get there more than once a year, they had made rolls for their own use in each house of God.

Je-sus came to Naz-a-reth where he had been brought up, and went in-to the church on the Lord's day and stood up to read. And he read from one of the old books where it was fore-told that one should come to bring good news to the poor, to cheer the sad, to give sight to the blind, and to heal the sick. Then he closed the roll and sat down. And the eyes of all in the church were on him. He said to them that all these words had come true, and that he was the Son of God, of whom the proph-et wrote. And they said, Is not this Jo-seph's son? How then can he claim to be the Son of God? And they were wroth with him, and led him out to a steep hill on which their town was built, that they might cast him down and kill him. But Je-sus got a-way from them, and they could do him no harm.

**TWO PA-GES of THE SAM-AR-I-TAN PENT-A-TEUCH.**

He went on to Ca-per-na-um, and great crowds came there to hear him, and pushed so that there was scarce room for him to stand on the sea-shore. And he saw two boats close at hand, out of which the men had gone to mend their nets. And he went in one of the boats, which was Pe-ter's and told him to push it out from the land. And he sat down, and taught the crowd out of the boat.

When he left off, he said to Pe-ter and An-drew, Sail out where the sea is deep, and let down your nets to catch fish.

Pe-ter said, Mas-ter, we have been hard at work all the night, and not a fish have we caught; but, since thou dost bid me, I will let down the net.

When they had done this, they caught such a large haul of fish that the net broke. Then they called to their friends in the boat by the shore, and bade them come to their aid. And they came, and there was more fish than the two boats could hold.

When Pe-ter saw this he fell down at the feet of Je-sus, and said, I fear thee, for I am full of sin, O Lord. And those with him were spell-bound at sight of the fish they had caught.

Je-sus did this great won-der so that these men might see it and know that he was the Son of God; for they were to aid him in his work, and to go with him from place to place.

Je-sus said to Pe-ter, Fear not; from this time forth thou shalt catch men and not fish. He meant by this that Pe-ter was to preach, and to save men from sin, and from the nets that Sa-tan spreads. And he said to them all, Come with me. And they left their boats and their nets, and all that they had, and were with Je-sus till the end of his life on earth.

**THE WON-DER-FUL DRAUGHT OF FISH-ES.**

On the Day of Rest, Je-sus went in-to the church and taught the folks there. And in their midst was a man who was not in his right mind, and it was as if he were torn by fiends, and he cried out to Je-sus, Let us a-lone. What have we to do with thee, thou Je-sus of Naz-a-reth? Art thou come to kill us? I know thee, that thou art the Son of God. Je-sus said to the fiends that were in the man, Be still, and come out of him. Then the fiends threw the man down, and cried with a loud voice, and came out of him. And all those in the church were struck with awe, and they said a-mong them-selves, What does this mean? for he speaks to the fiends so that they are forced to do his will!

When they came out of the church Je-sus went to the house where Pe-ter and An-drew dwelt. And James and John were there. And Pe-ter's wife's mo-ther was sick of a fe-ver, and they told Je-sus of it and begged that he would heal her.

Je-sus took her by the hand, and bade the fe-ver come out of her. And she was made well at once, and rose from her bed, and took charge of her house.

At the close of the day, when the sun had set, great crowds came to the house where Je-sus was, and brought those who were sick, and those who were not in their right minds, that he might cure them. And he made the sick well, and drove out the fiends, and would not let them speak.

The next day Je-sus rose ere it was light and went out to a lone place to pray to God.

**PE-TER'S WIFE'S MO-THER.**

For though he was the Son of God, he had come to the earth in the form of a man, and had all the wants that man has. He had need of food and drink, and felt pain and grief just as we do. He had need of man's help in his work; and had need of God's help all the time. And he knelt to God, just as he wants us to do, and asked God to be near him and to give him more strength, and to help him to do his will.

When Je-sus had gone, crowds came up to the house to seek him. And Peter, and the three that were with him, went out to look for Je-sus. And when they found him they told him of the great crowd that sought him.

Je-sus said, Let us go to the next towns, that I may tell the good news there; for I was not sent to stay in one place.

And he taught all through Gal-i-lee, and his fame spread, and great crowds went to hear him.

# CHAPTER VI.

## JESUS HEALS THE SICK, AND DOES GOOD WORKS ON THE DAY OF REST.

A man came to Je-sus and knelt down at his feet and said, Lord, if thou wilt thou canst make me clean. This man was a lep-er. He had white sores on his skin, and had to live by him-self or with those as bad off as him-self, and there was no cure for him but death. It was not safe to breathe the air near a lep-er, and so he was sent at once out of the town, as soon as his case was known.

**CUR-ING THE MAN LAME WITH PAL-SY.**

This lep-er must have heard of Je-sus and the great works he had done, and the hope that had died out must have sprung up in his heart once more. If he could heal the sick, and make the lame walk, why could he not cure him, so that he would be fit to live with those he loved? At least he could ask; and oh! how great must have been his faith when he fell down at the feet of Je-sus and cried out, Lord, if *thou* wilt *thou* canst make me clean.

Je-sus put out his hand and touched the man, and said, I will: be thou clean.

And at once the sores left the man and his skin was white and smooth. Then Je-sus sent him off, and bade him tell no man who had made him well, but to go to the priest and do as Mo-ses bid all those do who had been lep-ers and were cured.

But the man was so full of joy that he could not keep it to him-self, and he went out and told what Je-sus had done for him.

Now there were some Jews who were known as Scribes and Phar-i-sees. They made out that no one else was quite as good as they were. They knew all the laws of Mo-ses by heart, and they were strict to see that no Jews broke those laws. A Scribe is one who writes.

These Scribes and Phar-i-sees were thought to be wise and good men, for they would fast and pray for a long while at a time, and look as though they thought them-selves too pure for earth.

But their hearts were bad and full of sin, and when Je-sus told them they must give up their sins and lead the right kind of lives, they were wroth with him, and tried to make all the rest of the Jews hate him as much as they did.

Je-sus went down to Ca-per-na-um, and when it was known that he was in the town great crowds came to the house where he was to hear him preach.

Now there was a man who had been in bed for a long time, and could not move hand or foot. He had heard of the fame of Je-sus, and it was the wish of his heart to get near him that he might heal him with a touch. But Je-sus was a long way off, and the poor sick man could not walk one step. But he had kind friends, and they thought of a plan by which he could be brought near to Je-sus, that he might at least hear him preach.

So they took him on his bed and bore him to the town; but when they came to the house where Je-sus was, the crowd was so great that there was no chance to get near him. What were they to do?

Now the house was low and had a flat roof, with a wall round it, so that those who dwelt there could walk or sleep on it and have no fear that they would fall off. All the rooms down stairs led out in-to a court, which had a roof that could be slid off when it did not rain, or there was need of fresh air.

So the friends of the lame man drew the bed up on the house-top with him in it, and brought him to the space in the roof, through which they could see Je-sus and the crowds round him. And they let the man down on his bed in the midst of the crowd, which had to make way for him.

When Je-sus saw what great faith they had, he spoke to the sick man, and said, Thy sins are for-giv-en thee. Some of the Scribes and Phar-i-sees who sat near said, but not out loud, Who is this that dares speak in this way? None but God can for-give sins.

Je-sus knew their thoughts, and he said to them, Why think ye these things? Which could be said with the most ease, Thy sins be for-giv-en thee, or Rise up and walk?

But to show you that I have pow-er to for-give sins, I will make him well.

So he said to the sick man, Rise, take up thy bed, and go to thy house.

And the man rose and stood on his feet, and took up the bed on which he had lain and went out and gave praise and thanks to God.

And those who saw him were in a maze and said, We have seen strange things to-day.

Now the Jews, as you know, were slaves of the Ce-sar of Rome, and to keep their peace with him they had to pay a tax. And the men to whom they paid the tax were known as pub-li-cans. Some of them were harsh and stern, and the Jews could not but hate them. But all were not so. And as Je-sus went by he saw one of these pub-li-cans with his gold and sil-ver close at hand. His name was Matth-ew. Je-sus spoke to him, and said, Come with me.

And Matth-ew left all, and went with Je-sus, and from that time did all that he could to spread the good news, and to serve the Lord Christ.

**THE POOL OF BE-THES-DA.**

Af-ter this there was a feast of the Jews, and Je-sus went up to Je-ru-sa-lem. Now there was at Je-ru-sa-lem a pool, which was known as the Pool of Be-thes-da. And there were five courts, or door-ways, that led down to the pool. And in these courts lay a great crowd of folks who were sick, or blind, or lame.

For this was the time of the year when an an-gel came to stir the pool. And it was thought that the one who went in-to the pool the first, when the an-gel had made it fresh and sweet, would be cured of all the ails that he might have.

And a man was there who had been sick for most two-score years. Je-sus saw him, and knew that he had been sick for a long time, and it made him sad to think of it. So he said to the man, Wilt thou be made well?

The man said, I have no one to help me in-to the pool, for when I try to get down to it, some one steps in a-head of me and I am too late.

Je-sus said to him, Rise, take up thy bed and walk.

And at once the man was made well, and took up his bed, and walked.

Now it was the Day of Rest. And the Jews, who were quick to find fault with those who broke the laws, said to the man when he came their way, It is not right for thee to move thy bed on this day.

He said to them, he that made me well told me to take up my bed and walk.

They said to him, Who was it told thee that?

And the man did not know, and could not point Je-sus out to them, the crowd was so great.

But ere the feast was at an end Je-sus met the man He had cured and said to him, Now thou art well, sin no more lest a worse thing come to thee.

Then the man went out and told the Jews that it was Je-sus who had cured him on the Day of Rest. And for this the Jews sought to kill Je-sus. But he told them that the works he did were proof that God had sent him, and that he was the one of whom the seers had told in the days that were past, and of whom Mo-ses wrote.

## IN THE CORN-FIELDS.

He said that the time was near at hand when the dead should hear the voice of the Son of God, and those who were in their graves should come forth. Then he would judge them. Those who had done good would be blest, for God would give them a home with him in the sky; but those who had done ill, and died in their sins, would not meet the smile of God, nor have a place near his throne.

Je-sus said if the love of God was in their hearts they would trust him whom God had sent, and feel that he had come to do them good, and to save their souls from death.

Je-sus and his five friends, An-drew, Pe-ter, James, John, and Matth-ew, went out on the next Day of Rest, and their walk led them through a field of corn. And as the men had need of food, Je-sus told them to pluck and eat the ears of corn. And they did so.

In the East they gave the name of corn to all kinds of grain.

## THE WITH-ER-ED HAND.

When the Phar-i-sees saw it they found fault, and Je-sus told them that he was the best judge of what was right to do on that day; for he was Lord of the Day of Rest.

In the course of a few weeks he went in-to a church and taught on the Lord's day. And a man was there whose hand was so drawn up that he could not stretch it out or do aught with it. And the Phar-i-sees kept a close watch on Je-sus to see if he would heal the man on that day, so that they might find fault with them.

Je-sus knew their thoughts, and he said to the man with the lame hand, Rise up, and stand where all can see you. And the man rose, and stood forth.

**JER-U-SA-LEM.**

Je-sus said to them, I will ask you one thing: Is it right to do good or to do ill on the Day of Rest? to take life or to save it? And he stood and looked at all those that were in the place. Then he said to the man, Stretch out thy hand. And he did so, and it was well and strong.

This made the Phar-i-sees hate Je-sus, so that they went out of the church and sought for some way to put him to death. When he knew of it he left the place, and came down to the sea of Gal-i-lee. And crowds came to him from the land of Ju-dah and from large towns that were far off, to see the great works that he did. And the sick crept near so that they could touch him, and he made them all well.

# CHAPTER VII.

## THE SERMON ON THE MOUNT.

JE-SUS left the crowd, and went to a lone place to pray to God. And he spent the night there. The next morn he chose twelve men, that he might send them out to preach, and to heal those that were sick, and to cast out dev-ils. Their names were Pe-ter, An-drew, James and John, the sons of Zeb-e-dee, Phil-ip, Bar-thol-o-mew, Thom-as and Matth-ew, James and Leb-be-us, Si-mon and Ju-das Is-ca-ri-ot.

**THE SER-MON ON THE MOUNT.**

And the crowd was so great that Je-sus went up on a hill, and the twelve went with him and he taught them there. He told them that those who were in a high state of joy, with not a care to vex them, were called blest. And he said, not in these words, but in words that meant the same:

Blest are the poor in spirit, for God is with them.

By poor in spirit he meant those who did not think too much of them-selves, who were not vain nor proud, but rich in love to God. And he would be with them, and bless them all their lives.

Blest are those that mourn, for their tears shall be dried.

To mourn is to weep, and to grieve. Je-sus meant that those who wept for their sins should shed no more tears, for Christ had come to save them, and the good news should make them glad.

Blest are the meek, for the whole earth shall be theirs.

Je-sus meant by this that those who were fond of peace, and did not love strife, might dwell where they chose, and would be blest in this world and the world to come.

Blest are those who hun-ger and thirst for that which is good, for they shall be filled.

This meant that those who sought to do right and to grow in grace had but to pray to God, and he would give them all the strength they might need from day to day.

Blest are those who are kind and good, for the Lord will be kind to them in their hour of need.

Blest are those who are pure in heart, for they shall see God.

Those who are pure in heart will be fond of good works, and will lead good lives, and God will not turn his face from them.

Blest are the peace-ma-kers—those who try to keep the peace and to put an end to strife—for they shall be called the chil-dren of God.

Blest are those who are ill-used for my sake, for the more the world hates them the more will God love them.

Je-sus told them that when men said hard things of them for his sake, and called them vile, and were harsh with them and full of spite, they were not to grieve but to be glad. For so did bad men treat the seers of old who told them of their faults and their sins and tried to lead them to Christ.

Salt is good, and gives a taste to our food.

Je-sus told them they were to salt the earth. This meant that they were to tell the good news in such a way that men should want it and need it just as they did salt.

He told them, too, that they must let their light shine; he meant that they should let it be seen and known that they loved God, and tried to do his will. They were not to hide it from men, but to do such good works, in Christ's name, that those who did not love or care for him might be drawn to Je-sus—the light of the world.

Je-sus said that if we do as we ought to do our-selves, and teach men to keep all God's laws, we shall be called great in the place where God dwells. But if, like the Scribes and Phar-i-sees, we teach what is right and do what is wrong, we shall not see God's face, or live with him on high.

He said, you have been taught not to kill; and that he who puts one to death will be brought to the judge, and made to suf-fer for the crime. But I say to you that it is a sin to hate those who have done you no harm, and God will pun-ish you for it.

Then he said that when they went to church to wor-ship God they must try and think if they had done wrong, had been harsh, or had said what was not true. And they were to go at once and do right to those whom they hurt in this way, for God did not care to have them bow down to him if their hearts were full of sins they were not sor-ry for.

We must be good and pure, Je-sus says, in all that we say and do: we must do no harm to those who harm us, but must be kind and good to them, and pray for them, and love them.

Bless those that curse you, and do good to those that hate you. This is a hard task, and none but those who have the love of Christ in their hearts can do it. But if we pray for strength, the strength is sure to come, and love takes the place of hate.

Some folks when they do good deeds like to make a great show and noise, that they may be seen of men, and have much praise from them.

Je-sus told the Twelve that they were to do right, not to please men but to please God. When they gave to the poor they were not to tell of it; and when they prayed they were not to choose a place where they could be seen of men—just to show how good they were—but were to go to their room and shut the door, that no one but God could hear them. Then God would give them what they asked for.

Je-sus taught them how to pray, and what words to use; and these words each child ought to learn by heart and use at least twice a day:

"Our Fa-ther which art in heav-en, Hal-low-ed be thy name. Thy King-dom come. Thy will be done on earth as *it is* in heav-en. Give us this day our dai-ly bread. And for-give us our debts, as we for-give our debt-ors. And lead us not in-to tempt-a-tion, but del-iv-er us from e-vil: For thine is the King-dom, and the pow-er, and the glo-ry, for ever. *A-men.*"

When they should fast they were not to look sad as those did whose wish it was that men should see them fast, but they were to hold up their heads and wear a look of cheer that no one but God should know it. And God would bless them for it.

Je-sus said we must not want to be rich or to lay up wealth in this world, for when we die we can-not take it with us. But we should give our hearts to thoughts of God, and try to live so that we can share his home, where we shall have more things to please us than all the gold in the world can buy.

Je-sus said that no man could serve God and serve Sa-tan too. We serve God when we do right; and we serve Sa-tan when we do wrong.

So we can-not do the will of both, and must choose which one we will serve.

He told the Twelve not to judge folks; he meant that they must take care how they found fault, and blamed them. For they may not have done wrong, or if they did they may have meant no harm. We can-not see men's hearts, or know how they felt at the time they did the deed. But God knows all, and may not blame them as much as we do. Je-sus said that we should strive to do right our-selves, and then we should see with clear eyes who did wrong, and have a right to tell them of their faults.

He said, that what we want men to do to us we must do to them. If we want them to be kind and good and to treat us well, we must do the same by them.

**THE UN-FRUIT-FUL TREE.**

He said, Strive to go in at the strait, or nar-row gate; for wide is the gate and broad is the way that leads to death. He meant that the good and the bad ways are like two gates in our path, for us to choose which one we will go through.

The good way is small and hard to find, and we have to search for it with great care. But the path is one that leads to life and joy.

The bad way is like a broad gate that stands o-pen and in plain sight. This wide gate leads down to hell, and crowds and crowds go that way, while but few are found in the good way that leads to bliss.

Je-sus said that at the last day some would call him Lord, Lord, and say they had served him and taught as he did. But he would say that he did not know them, for they had bad hearts, and had led lives of sin, and were not fit to dwell with the good and pure in the home on high, where all is love.

He said that men were like trees. Good trees brought forth good fruit; but a bad tree could not bring forth good fruit. And men were to be known by their works, just as a tree was known by its fruits.

Then he spoke of two men, each of whom built a house. One chose to build on a rock. And the rain fell, and the floods came, and the winds blew and beat on that house, but it stood firm and the storm did it no harm.

But one of the men built his house on the sand. And the rain fell, and the floods came, and the winds blew and beat on that house, and it fell with a great crash, and was swept out of sight.

Je-sus said that those who heard his words and did as he told them were like the wise man who built his house on a rock. Christ is our Rock. He stands firm. No storms can move him. If we cling to him he will save us.

Je-sus said that those who heard his words and did not do as he taught them, were like the man who built his house on the sand. When the storm came on the last day, when God would judge the world, they would be swept out of sight. And oh! what a sad, sad day that will be for all those who have led bad lives, and done not the least thing to please God, who took care of them and gave them all they had.

We must strive to be good all the time, and to love Je-sus, so that he will be near us, and will take us home to live with him when we die.

# CHAPTER VIII.

## GOOD WORDS AND GOOD WORKS.

THERE was at Ca-per-na-um a chief who had charge of five score Ro-man troops. And one of his men, who was dear to him, was so sick that he was like to die. When the chief heard that Je-sus was there he sent some of his friends down to ask him to make the sick man well. Those who brought the word to Je-sus were Jews, and they spoke a good word for the chief, who had been kind to them.

Then Je-sus went with them. But as they drew near the chief's house he sent some more friends out to tell Je-sus that he had not gone down to him himself, for he was not good e-nough. And now he sent word that he was not good e-nough for Je-sus to come in-to his house. But if Je-sus would speak the word, he was sure that the sick man would get well.

**CHRIST AND THE CEN-TU-RI-ON.**

For I stand at the head of my troops, said the chief, and say to this one, Go, and he goes; and to that one, Come, and he comes; and to a third, Do this, and he does it.

And he knew that if he could do this Je-sus could do more, and bid all the ills leave the sick man at the sound of his voice.

When Je-sus heard these words he was a-mazed, and said to those who were with him, I have found no one who has such faith in me as this Ro-man. And I tell you that at the last day those who have had faith in me shall come from all lands, and have a place near God's throne; while the Jews, who will not put their trust in me, will be shut out.

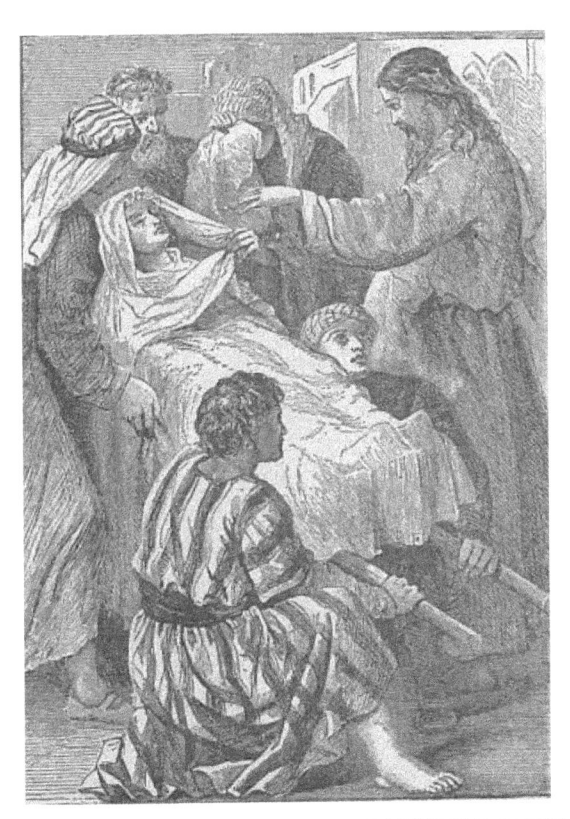

**THE WID-OW'S SON BROUGHT TO LIFE.**

And when the friends of the chief went back they found the sick man made well.

The next day Je-sus went to the town of Nain. And a great crowd went with him. And as they came near the gate of the town they saw a dead man brought out to be borne to his grave. He was all the son his mo-ther had, and her friends stood near her and wept with her.

When Je-sus saw her grief his heart was sad, and he said, Weep not.

And he came up to the bier on which the dead lay, and those who bore it stood still. Then Je-sus said, Young man, I say to thee a-rise.

And he that was dead sat up and spoke. And Je-sus gave him to his mo-ther. And a great fear came on all who saw it, and they gave praise to God, and said that a great proph-et had been raised up in their midst.

In old times those who lived in the East did not wear shoes such as we do. They wore light soles, or san-dals, which were bound on their feet with straps, and thrown off as soon as they came in-to the house. Then wa-ter was brought for them to wash their feet.

Much oil was used in those lands, and is to this day. It was put on the hair to keep it moist, and on the skin to make it soft and smooth. This oil, when some-what hard, was called oint-ment, and was kept in a box, and had a nice smell.

Now a Phar-i-see, whose name was Si-mon, asked Je-sus to his house. And Je-sus went there, and they sat down to eat. And a wo-man of the town, who had led a life of sin, when she heard that Je-sus was there, came in with a box of oint-ment and bowed down at his feet.

She was full of shame, for her sins had been great, and she had come to Je-sus to ask him to for-give her and help her to lead a new life.

She wept, and washed the feet of Je-sus with her tears, and wiped them with the hairs of her head. And she kissed his feet, and rubbed them with the oint-ment she had brought, and which had cost her a high price.

When the Phar-i-see saw it he said to him-self, If this man had come from God he would know what kind of a wo-man this is, and would send her out of his sight.

Je-sus, who knew his every thought, said to him, Si-mon, I have some-thing to say to thee.

**WASH-ING HANDS IN THE EAST.**

And he said, My lord, say on.

Then Je-sus said, Two men were in debt to a rich man. One owed him a great deal, while the oth-er owed him but a small sum. But they were both so poor that they could not pay him, and he told them to think no more of the debt, for it would be the same as if they had paid all they owed. Tell me now which one of these would love him the most.

The Phar-i-see said, I should think that he to whom he for-gave the most.

Je-sus said to him, That is true.

And he turned to the wo-man and said to Si-mon, See'st thou this wo-man? I came to thy house, and thou didst bring me no wa-ter to wash my feet, but she hath washed my feet with her tears and wiped them with the hairs of her head. Thou didst give me no kiss, but this wo-man, since the time I came in, has not ceased to kiss my feet. My head with oil thou didst not an-oint, but she has poured her oint-ment on my feet. So I say to thee that her sins, though so great, will be all wiped out, for she has loved me much.

And he said to the wo-man, Thy faith has saved thee; go back to thy home in peace.

From this place Je-sus went on through all the large and small towns, and told the good news that God had sent his Son in-to the world to save men from their sins. And the twelve were with him.

Je-sus might have been rich, for all the world was his; but he chose to be poor, and to bear all the ills of life for our sakes, that we might be drawn to him, and be saved from our sins. Good wo-men, whom he had cured, gave him such things as he had need of, and he did not lack for food or friends.

Je-sus spoke at times in a strange way. He would take scenes from real life and paint them, as it were, with words, so that they were plain to all. These talks were meant to teach great truths that would lodge in the mind, and stand out like scenes of real life. They were to take them home with them, and keep them in their thoughts from day to day.

One of these talks was of a rich man who had large fields and vine-yards. And when it was time for the crops to come in, the rich man found that his barns would not hold them.

And he said, What shall I do? for I have no room where I can put my fruits. This will I do: I will pull down my small barns and build large ones, and there will I store all my goods. And I will say to my-self, Thou hast much goods laid up that will last thee for years and years; take thine ease, eat, drink, and be of good cheer.

But God said to him, Thou fool, this night thou shalt die. Then who shall have those things which thou hast laid up for years to come?

This was to teach us that it is of no use for men to lay up great wealth in this world, for they will have to leave it all when they die. And it is a sin for a rich man to spend all that he owns on him-self, to live at his ease, and to eat and drink, as if there were no poor in the world, and no God to serve.

Je-sus told the twelve not to fret be-cause they were poor, or to have the least fear that they might want for food, or for clothes to wear. Think of the birds, he said. They do not sow seed in the fields, nor reap grain and lay it up for use in time of need. They have no store-house or barn, yet they have all the food they want, for God feeds them and takes care of them. And if he does so much for the birds, how much more will he do for you?

Look at the flow-ers. See how they grow. They do not work, or spin the thread to weave in-to cloth as men must do, and yet I say to you that King Sol-o-mon did not wear such rich robes as theirs. If then God gives such fine clothes to that which grows in the field like grass, and which in a day or two is burnt up, how much more will he clothe you, though ye are so loth to trust him. So do not fret lest you shall want for things to eat, and to drink, and to wear; for God knows that ye have need of these things, and if ye seek first to do his will, he will give all these things to you.

# CHAPTER IX.

## JESUS AT THE SEA-SHORE.

WHILE Je-sus was down by the sea, the crowd grew so great that he went in-to a boat and sat down to teach them as they stood on the shore.

**THE SOW-ER.**

He said, A man went out in the field to sow his seed. And as he threw the seed from his hand, some of it fell on the hard path by the road-side, and the birds flew down and ate it. Some fell on the rocks and stones where there was not much earth, and it soon grew up on top of the ground. But the sun's warm rays made it droop, and as it had no root, in a few days it was all dried up.

Some of the seed fell where thorns and weeds were, and these took up all the room, so that there was no space for the seed to grow. The air and the sun could not get at it, and soon it was choked to death.

But some of the seed fell in good ground, that the plough had made soft. The rain fell on it, the sun shone on it, and it sprang up and bore a large crop of grain.

When the crowd had left Je-sus, the twelve came near to ask him what he had meant to teach by this talk of seeds that were sown here and there.

Je-sus told them the seed was the good news that he came to preach. Those who preach, or teach, sow good or bad seed, which takes root in the mind or heart.

Some who heard his words would not care for them, but would go on in their sins and feel no change of heart. New thoughts and fresh scenes would come and eat up the seed-thoughts that Je-sus had sown, as quick as the birds ate up the seed sown by the road-side.

Some who heard him thought of his words for a-while, and tried for a short time to do right. But it did not last long. This was the seed that fell in the midst of stones, and sprang up at first, but in a few days was all dried up.

**THE EN-E-MY SOW-ING TARES.**

Some would hear Je-sus preach, and were glad of the words that he spoke; but the cares of this world, their wealth, and the gay things of life, were so much in their thoughts that they could not do the things he had taught them.

This was the seed that fell in the midst of thorns, and the thorns grew up and choked it.

But there were some who heard Je-sus preach, and who tried each day to do as he taught them. This was the seed that fell in good ground, which took root and grew and brought forth ten times as much as had been sown.

One of the talks of Je-sus was of a man who sowed good seed in his field. And while he slept a foe came and sowed tares, or weeds, in the midst of the wheat, and then went on his way. And when it was time for the wheat to grow up, the weeds grew up with it.

And when the work-men on the farm saw this, they went at once to the man of the house, and said to him, Didst thou not sow good seed in thy field? Where then have these tares come from?

He said to them, A foe has done this.

The work-men said, Shall we go out, then, and pull them up by the roots?

And he said, No, lest while you pull up the tares you pull up the wheat with them. Let both grow till it is time to reap the grain; and then I will say to the reap-ers, Pull up the tares first and bind them in stacks to burn. But put the wheat in my barn.

Je-sus told the twelve what he meant by this talk of the tares of the field.

The field is the world. He who owns the field and sows the seed, is Je-sus him-self. The wheat that grows up means those who hear his words, and do as he has taught them.

The tares are bad men, who have no love for Je-sus.

The foe that sows them is Sa-tan.

The time to reap the grain is on the last great day. The reap-ers are the an-gels.

Je-sus will let the good and the bad live in the world till the last great day. Then he will send his an-gels to take the good to their home on high, but the bad will be cast out in-to the fire that is to burn up the world.

**SEEK-ING GREAT PEARLS.**

Then Je-sus spoke of a man who went out to buy pearls. He went from place to place, and those who had pearls to sell brought them out for him to look at, but he was hard to suit, and bought but few. At last he found one that was worth more than all the rest that he had seen. But its price was so great that he could not buy it. What did he do? Why, he went and sold all that he had, and came back and bought this pearl of great price.

So will it be with those who wish to be rid of their sins, and to be as pure as a pearl with-in. Je-sus in us is the pearl of great price. Gold can-not buy it. But when we learn its cost we should make haste to get rid of all that keeps Christ out of our hearts, and make room for this one pearl, which is worth more than all else in the world.

Then Je-sus spoke of those who took their net, and went out in a boat to catch fish. They cast thenet out of the boat and threw it in-to the sea, and when it was full drew it back to shore. Then they sat down to sort the fish; the good ones were put in their boats, and the bad ones were thrown a-way.

**PAR-A-BLE OF THE NETS.**

So it would be at the last day. The an-gels would come forth and sort the good from the bad. And the good would be borne to their home on high, but the bad would be thrown in-to a fire that would make them cry out with pain.

Je-sus said, Have I made these things plain to thee? And they said, Yes, Lord.

One of the Scribes came to Je-sus, and said, I will not leave thee; but where thou dost go I will go. Je-sus said to him, The fox-es have holes, and the birds of the air have nests, but I have not where to lay my head. He meant by this that he was poor, and had no place wherehe could go and lie down when he had need of rest.

**STILL-ING THE TEM-PEST.**

Night drew near, and the crowd was so great that Je-sus and the twelve went in a boat to cross the Sea of Gal-i-lee. And there came up a great storm, and the winds blew fierce, and the waves rose high and came with a great dash in-to the boat.

And Je-sus slept, for he was quite worn out. The twelve were full of fear; and at last they woke Je-sus, and said, Lord, save us, or we shall sink.

Then he rose and spoke to the winds and the waves, and said to them, Peace, be still. And the wind ceased to blow, and soon all was still and calm.

And Je-sus said to the twelve, Why are ye in such fear? How is it that ye have no faith?

As Je-sus left the boat a mad-man came out of the tombs to meet him. He was so fierce that no mancould bind him, or tame him. He broke loose from all the ropes and chains, and no house could hold him. So night and day he would roam on the hills and in the caves or tombs, where graves had been dug, and cry out and cut him-self with bits of stones.

And while Je-sus was still far off, the mad-man saw him and ran and fell down at his feet. And he cried out, What have I to do with thee, Je-sus, thou Son of God? Harm me not, I pray thee.

Now there was there, close by the hills, a great herd of swine. And the fiends that were in the man begged Je-sus to send them in-to the swine. And Je-sus said, Go. And when they came out of the man they went in the swine, and the herd ran down a steep place and were drowned in the sea.

And they that fed the swine went and told what had been done, and great crowds came to the place where Je-sus was.

And when they saw that the mad-man sat with his clothes on and in his right mind, they were in great fear. And they prayed Je-sus to leave the place at once.

When Je-sus was come in-to the boat, he that had been out of his mind begged that he might go with him. But Je-sus would not let him, and said to him, Go home to thy friends, and tell them what great things the Lord hath done for thee.

And the man went and told how he had been made well, and those who heard him felt that Je-sus must have been sent from God, for no mere man could do such strange things.

# CHAPTER X.

## JESUS BRINGS THE DEAD TO LIFE.—FEEDS FIVE THOUSAND.

Je-sus went back to Ca-per-na-um. And as he stood by the sea-shore, one of the chief men of the church came to him, whose name was Ja-i-rus.

He was in deep grief, for he had but one child, a girl twelve years of age, and she lay sick at his home and there was no help for her. And he said to Je-sus, My child lies at the point of death. I pray thee come and lay thy hands on her that she may live.

And Je-sus went with him, and so did the twelve, and all the crowd that had come up to hear Je-sus preach. And in the throng was a wo-man who had been sick for twelve years. She had spent all she had to try to be made well; but all the drugs she took did her no good, and no one could seem to help her case. So she went on from bad to worse.

When she heard of Je-sus she came up with the crowd at his back, and put out her hand and touched the hem of his robe. For, she said, if I may touch but his clothes I shall be made well. And as soon as she had done this she felt that she was cured.

All this was known to Je-sus, and yet he faced the crowd and said, Who touched me?

Pe-ter said that some one in the throng had been pushed up close to him and thought it strange that Je-sus did not know it.

Je-sus said, Someone touched me, and he looked round to see who had done it.

When the wo-man saw that Je-sus knew all, and that she could not hide from him, she shook with fear, and fell down at his feet, and told him why she had touched him, and how that touch had made her well.

Je-sus said to her, Be of good cheer. Thy faith in me hath made thee well.

While he yet spoke to her, there came one from the house of Ja-i-rus, who said to him, Thy child is dead.

When Je-sus heard it he said, Fear not. Trust in me and she shall be made well. And when he came to the house, he found a great crowd there, who wept and mourned the loss of the young child.

Je-sus said to them, Why do you weep? She sleeps; she is not dead.

He meant that she would soon rise from the dead, as one who wakes out of his sleep.

**CUR-ED BY TOUCH-ING HIS GAR-MENT.**

But they saw that she was dead, and as they had no faith in his words they laughed him to scorn.

Then he put them all out of the room save three of the twelve—Pe-ter, James, and John—and the fa-ther and mo-ther of the young girl. Then he took the child by the hand and said, I say to thee a-rise. And she rose from her bed, and had strength to walk, and Je-sus bade them bring her some food that she might eat.

And her fa-ther and mo-ther knew not what to think of these strange things. Je-sus bade them tell no one of what he had done, and there was no need for them to speak. For there was their child, well and strong, once more the light and joy of their house, and their hearts must have been full of thanks and praise to God!

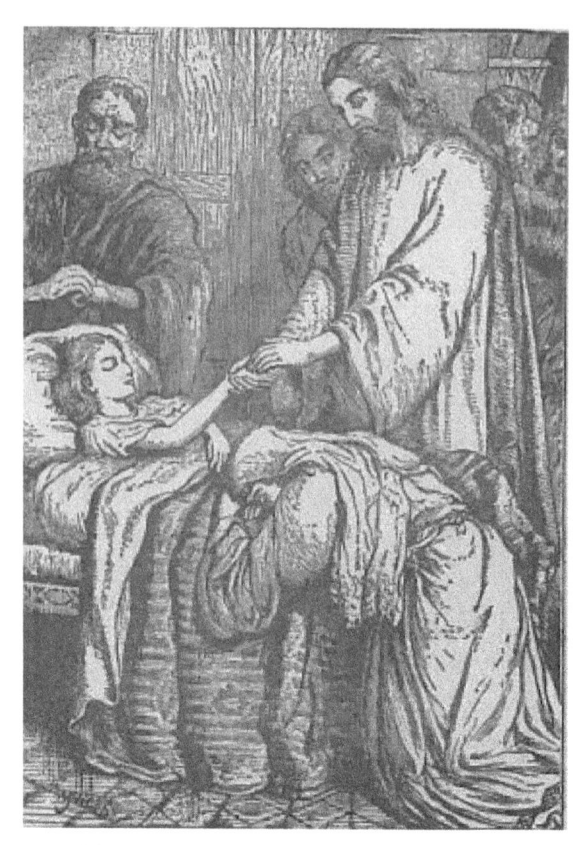

## THE DAU-GHTER OF JA-I-RUS.

When Je-sus went from the house of Ja-i-rus two blind men came near him and cried out, Thou Son of Da-vid have mer-cy on us. They said this be-cause they knew that he was of King Da-vid's race.

Je-sus said to them, Do you think that I can make you well? They said to him, Yes, Lord.

Then he touched their eyes, and at once their sight came back to them. And he said to them, Tell no man what I have done to you. But when they left him they went from place to place and told all whom they met how Je-sus had brought back their sight.

And they brought to him a dumb man who could not speak be-cause of the fiend that was in him. Andas soon as Je-sus cast out the fiend the man spoke. And all those who saw it were in a maze, and said, Such things as these have not been done be-fore in the land of Is-ra-el.

**THE TWO BLIND MEN.**

But the Phar-i-sees felt such hate for Je-sus that they said that he could cast out fiends be-cause he had the help of Sa-tan, the prince of all fiends.

Je-sus said to the twelve, Come, let us go to some lone place and rest a while. For the crowds were so great that they had no time to eat. And they went in a boat quiet-ly to cross the Sea of Gal-i-lee, where they might rest and take the food they were so much in need of. But as soon as the folks heard of it they set out on foot and went round by the shore till they came to the place where Je-sus was.

And when Je-sus went out and saw them, his heart was moved, and he taught them, and made the sick ones well.

When night came on, the twelve said to Je-sus, Send these off that they may go to the towns and buy food for them-selves, for they have nought to eat.

Je-sus said, They need not go. Give you them some-thing to eat.

They said, Shall we go out and buy bread and give it to them?

Je-sus said, How much have you? Go and see.

When they knew they said, We have five loaves and two small fish-es.

Je-sus bade the twelve have the crowd seat them-selves in rows on the green grass. Then he took the five loaves and the two fish-es, and gave thanks to God for them. And he broke the loaves, and the fish-es, and the twelve gave them piece by piece to the crowd, till all had had their fill.

When the feast was at an end there was e-nough bread and fish left to fill twelve bas-kets.

Then Je-sus bade the twelve dis-ci-ples get in-to the boat and go back to Ca-per-na-um.

And when the crowd had left him he went up on a high hill to pray. And when night came on he was there with none but God near him.

**FEED-ING THE MUL-TI-TUDE.**

The twelve were in the boat, out in the midst of the sea.

Their oars were of no use, for the wind blew hard the wrong way, and drove them back from their course, and made the waves toss the boat here and there.

Je-sus could see it all from his high place on the hill, and in the night he went down to the shore and walked out on the sea.

When the twelve saw him they were in a great fright, for they thought it was a ghost, and they cried out in their fear.

Je-sus said, Be of good cheer. It is I.

Pe-ter spoke from the boat, and said, Lord, if it be thou, bid me come to thee on the sea. Je-sus said to him, Come, and Pe-ter came out of the boat and walked on the waves to go to Je-sus. But when he heard the noise of the wind, and saw the waves dash all round him, he was in great fear; and as he felt him-self sink he cried out, Lord, save me.

**PE-TER WALK-ING ON THE WA-TER.**

Je-sus put forth his hand and caught him, and said to him, O thou of lit-tle faith, why didst thou doubt me?

When Je-sus and Pe-ter came in-to the boat the wind was still, and the twelve were soon on the shore they had set out to reach. Then they fell at his feet, and said, It is true that thou art the Son of God.

**CHRIST WALK-ING ON THE SEA.**

As soon as it was known where Je-sus was, crowds came from all the towns that were near, and brought their sick in their beds that he might make them well. And when he went through the large and small towns they laid the sick in the streets, and begged that they might touch but the hem of his robe. And at a touch they were all made well.

# CHAPTER XI.

## JESUS HEALS THE SICK.—HIS FORM CHANGED ON THE MOUNT.

JE-SUS went to Ca-per-na-um and taught the Jews there. But all that he said made them hate him the more, and their chief priests did all they could to prove that he was not the Christ who was to save them. They thought that he who was to be the King of the Jews would come in rich robes, and with all the signs of high rank. So they would have naught to do with a poor man like Je-sus.

It made Je-sus sad to have the Jews turn from him, and he left them, and went out to the towns of Tyre and Si-don, which were on the sea-coast. And no Jews dwelt there.

Yet a wo-man, as soon as she heard he was there, came out and cried to him, O Lord, thou Son of Da-vid, come and heal my child, for she has gone mad.

**THE AS-CEN-SION.**

Je-sus said he was sent to none but the Jews. This he did to try her faith, for she was not a Jew.

But she fell at his feet, and cried out, Lord help me!

**SI-DON.**

Je-sus said to her, Great is thy faith; thy child is made well.

And when she went back to her house she found her child had been made well at the same hour that she spoke to Je-sus.

Then Je-sus and the twelve went down near the Sea of Gal-i-lee once more. And they brought to Je-sus a man that was deaf, and who could not speak plain, that he might lay his hands on him and heal him.

Je-sus took him out of the crowd, and touched his ears and tongue, and at once the man was made well, so that he could both hear and speak.

And crowds came to him, and brought those that were lame, blind, and dumb, and laid them down at the feet of Je-sus, that he might heal them. And Je-sus healed them all, so that the crowds were in a maze when they saw the dumb speak, the lame walk, and the blind see; and they gave praise and thanks to God for what he had done.

At the end of six days Je-sus took Pe-ter, James, and John, and went up on a high mount to pray. And while he was there a great change took place in him. His face shone as the sun, and his clothes were as white as snow, and the light shone through them.

And Mo-ses and E-li-jah came to him, and spoke with him.

Pe-ter said, Lord, it is good for us to be here. Let us make three tents, one for thee, and one for Mo-ses, and one for E-li-jah.

While he yet spoke there came a bright cloud, out of which a voice spoke and said, This is my dear Son, in whom I am well pleased. Hear ye him.

When Pe-ter, James, and John heard it, they bowed down to the ground, and were in great fear.

Je-sus came and touched them, and said, Rise. Fear not. And when they raised their eyes they saw no one but Je-sus.

As they came down from the mount, Je-sus bade them tell no one what they had seen till he rose from the dead.

**PE-TER AND THE TRIB-UTE MON-EY.**

The next day, when they had come down from the mount, there was a great crowd to see Je-sus. And one man knelt at his feet and said, Lord, help my son, for he has fits, and the fiends in him vex him so that he falls in the fire and in the wa-ter. I took him to those whom thou hast taught to heal, to see if they could cure him; and they could not.

Je-sus said, Bring him to me. And they brought him; and he fell on the ground and foamed at the mouth.

Je-sus said to the fiend that was in the young man, Come out of him and vex him no more.

And the fiend cried with a loud voice, and shook the young man, and came out of him, but left him weak, like one dead. And those who stood near thought he was dead. But Je-sus took him by the hand and raised him, and he stood on his feet and was well from that hour.

Then Je-sus and the twelve went to Ca-per-na-um. And when they were in the house Je-sus said, Why were ye at such strife in your talk on the way?

And for shame they held their peace, for their talk had been as to which should have the high-est place in the realm where Je-sus was to reign as King of the Jews.

When they had sat down Je-sus said to the twelve, He who seeks to be first shall be last of all.

And he took a child and set it in the midst of them, and told them that they must put pride out of their hearts and be as meek as a child. For he who thought not of him-self, but did God's will as a child does the will of its fa-ther, the same should be great in the realm which Je-sus was to set up.

Je-sus taught there for some time, and then setout for Je-ru-sa-lem. And the twelve went with him.

When they were come to Ca-per-na-um, those that took in the trib-ute mon-ey came to Pe-ter and said, Doth not your mas-ter pay trib-ute.

This was the tax the Jews had to pay to Ce-sar as the price of peace.

Pe-ter said, Yes. And when he came in-to the house Je-sus met him and said.

Of whom do the kings of the earth take cus-tom or trib-ute? of their own chil-dren or of stran-gers?

Pe-ter said, Of stran-gers.

Je-sus said, Then are the chil-dren free. But lest we should give cause for blame, go thou to the sea, and cast a hook, and take up the fish that first comes up. In its mouth thou shalt find a piece of mon-ey. Take that and give it to them for me and thee.

# CHAPTER XII.

## THE GOOD SAMARITAN.—MARTHA AND MARY.—THE MAN BORN BLIND.

JE-SUS went to the great church in Je-ru-sa-lem, and the Jews came there in crowds to hear him preach, and to find fault with him.

And a man of law stood up and said, What must I do to be saved? Je-sus said to him, What does the law say? How dost thou read it? The man of law said, Thou shalt love the Lord thy God with all thy heart, and with all thy soul, and with all thy strength, and thy neigh-bor as thy-self.

Je-sus said to him, That is right. Do this, and thou shalt be saved.

The man of law said, Who is my neigh-bor? Then Je-sus spoke in this way, and said, A man went down from Je-ru-sa-lem to Je-ri-cho. And the thieves fell on him, tore off his clothes and beat him, then went on their way and left him half dead on the ground.

By chance there came a priest that way, and when he saw the poor man he went by him on the oth-er side of the road.

Then one of the tribe of Le-vi came to the place, and took a look at the poor man, and went by on the oth-er side of the road.

By and by a Sa-mar-i-tan—that is, a man from Sa-ma-ri-a—came that way, and as soon as he saw the poor man on the ground his heart was moved, and he made haste to help him.

**THE GOOD SAM-AR-I-TAN.**

Now the Jews did not like the Sa-mar-i-tans, and would have nought to do with them. And those to whom Je-sus spoke would not have thought it strange if this man from Sa-ma-ri-a had left the Jew to die by the road-side.

But this he could not do, for he had a kind heart. He went to the poor man and bound up his wounds, and set him on his own beast, and brought him to an inn, and took care of him.

And the next day when he left he took out two pence and gave them to the host, and said to him, Take care of him; and if thou hast need to spend more than that, when I come back I will pay thee.

Which now of these three dost thou think was neigh-bor to him who fell a-mong thieves?

And the man of law said, He that was kind to him.

Then said Je-sus, Go, and do thou like-wise; that is, to those who need help go and do as the Sa-mar-i-tan did.

Je-sus came to Beth-a-ny—a small place near Je-ru-sa-lem—and a wo-man, whose name was Mar-tha, asked him to come to her house. She had a sis-ter, whose name was Ma-ry, and while Mar-tha went to get things and to cook, and sweep, and dust, Ma-ry sat down at the feet of Je-sus to hear him talk.

This did not please Mar-tha, who felt that she had too much work to do; so she came to Je-sus and said, Lord, dost thou not care that my sis-ter hath left me to do the work a-lone? Bid her there-fore come and help me.

Je-sus said to her, Mar-tha, Mar-tha, thou art full of care and vexed a-bout more things than there is need of. There is need of but one thing, and Ma-ry hath made choice of that which is good, and no one shall take it from her.

He meant that Ma-ry chose to care for her soul, and to be taught how to live in this world, so that she might fit her-self for the next one. And the one thing we all need is a new heart, full of love to Je-sus and glad to do his work.

One of the twelve said to Je-sus, Teach us how to pray, as John taught those who were with him. Je-sus taught them to pray thus:

## MA-RY AND MAR-THA.

Our Fa-ther, who art in heav-en, Hal-low-ed be thy name, Thy king-dom come, Thy will be done on earth as it is in heav-en, Give us this day our dai-ly bread, and for-give us our debts as we for-give our debt-ors. Lead us not in-to temp-ta-tion but de-liv-er us from e-vil, for thine is the king-dom, the pow-er, and the glo-ry, both now and for-ev-er. A-men.

Then he said, Which of you shall have a friend and shall go to him at mid-night and say to him, Friend, lend me three loaves: for a friend of mine has come a long way to see me, and I have no food for him.

And he who is in-side shall say, The door is now shut, and my chil-dren are with me in bed; I can-not rise and give thee.

I say to you, though he will not rise and give him be-cause he is his friend, yet if he keeps on and begs hard he will rise and give him as much as he needs. And I say to you, Ask God for what you need and he will give it to you. Seek and ye shall find. Knock, and the door that is shut will o-pen for you.

For, he said, if a child of yours should ask for bread, would you give him a stone? or should he ask for a fish, would you give him a snake? If ye then, who are full of sin, know how to give good gifts to your chil-dren, how much more sure is it that God will give good things to those who ask him.

Je-sus chose three-score and ten more men and sent them out, two and two, in-to all the towns where he meant to come, that they might heal the sick and preach the good news. And they did as he told them, and came back full of joy at the great things they had done through the strength that he gave them. Je-sus told them that they should feel more joy that their names were set down in the Book of Life—God's book—where he keeps the names of all those who love him, and do his will on earth.

**THE SEND-ING OUT OF THE SEV-EN-TY.**

The Feast of Tents was near at hand, and Je-sus said to the twelve, Go ye up to this feast, but Iwill not go now, for my time has not yet come. So he staid in Gal-i-lee for a-while. Then he went up to Je-ru-sa-lem, but did not make him-self known lest the Jews should kill him.

The Jews sought for him at the feast, and said, Where is he? And there was much talk of him. Some said, He is a good man; and some said, No, he is a fraud. But no one dared to speak well of him out loud for fear of the Jews.

In the midst of the feast Je-sus went up in-to the church and taught there. And he said, Ye both know me, and ye know from whence I came. I am not come to please my-self, but to do the will of him that sent me, whom ye know not. But I know him, for I have come from him, and he hath sent me.

Then they made a rush for him, but no man laid hands on him, for his hour had not yet come. God had set the time for him to die, and no one could harm him till that day and hour.

As he came from the church he saw a man who had been blind from his birth. Je-sus spat on the ground and made clay of the moist earth, and spread the clay on the eyes of the blind man.

Then he told him to go and wash in a pool that was near. And he went, and did as he was told, and his sight came back to him.

And his friends, and those who had seen him when he was blind, said, Is not this he that sat and begged?

**"ONCE I WAS BLIND, BUT NOW I SEE."**

Some said, This is he; and some said, He is like him; but the man said, I am he.

Then they said to him, How were thine eyes cured?

And he said, A man, by the name of Je-sus, made clay and spread it on my eyes, and said to me, Go to the pool of Si-lo-am and wash; and I went and did so, and my sight came back to me.

Then they said to him, Where is he? He said, I know not.

It was on the day of rest that Je-sus made the clay, and the Phar-i-sees, when they heard of it, said, This man is not of God, for he does not keep the day of rest. And they went to the fa-ther and the mo-therof the man who had been blind, and said to them, Is this your son, who ye say was born blind? How then doth he now see?

His pa-rents said, We know that this is our son, and that he was born blind; but by what means he now sees, or who hath cured his eyes, we know not. He is of age, ask him; he shall speak for him-self.

They spoke thus for fear of the Jews; for the Jews had made it known that all those who said that Je-sus was the Christ should be put out of the church. So they said, He is of age; ask him.

Then the Phar-i-sees went to the man that was blind, and said to him, Give God the praise, for we know that this man is a man of sin.

He said to them, What he is I know not; but this I do know, that once I was blind, but now I see.

Then they said to him, What did he do to thee? How did he cure thine eyes?

The man said, I have told you be-fore, and ye did not hear. Why would ye hear me say it once more? Would ye be of his band?

Then they spoke harsh words to him, and said, Thou dost take sides with him, but we stand by Mo-ses. We know that God spoke to Mo-ses; but as for this fel-low, we know not who sent him.

The man said, It is strange that ye know not who sent him, when he has brought sight to my blindeyes. Since the world was made we have not heard of a man who could give sight to one that was born blind. If this man were not of God he could not have done this thing.

The Phar-i-sees were full of wrath, and said to the man, Thou hast dwelt in sin from thy birth, and wilt thou try to teach us? And they drove him out of the church.

Je-sus heard of it, and when he found the man he said to him, Have you faith in the son of God?

He said, Who is he, Lord, that I may put my trust in him?

Je-sus said, It is he that talks with thee.

The man said, Lord, I know that it must be so; and he fell at the feet of Je-sus, and gave praise to him.

# CHAPTER XIII.

## JESUS, THE GOOD SHEPHERD.—LAZARUS BROUGHT TO LIFE.—THE FEAST, AND THOSE WHO WERE BID TO IT.

JE-SUS said to those whom he taught, I am the good shep-herd. The good shep-herd will give his life for the sheep. But he that is hired, and who does not own the sheep, when he sees the wolf will leave the sheep and run to save his own life. Then the wolf lays hold of the sheep, and puts the flock to flight. He who is hired flees from the sheep, be-cause he does not care for them.

I am the good shep-herd and know my sheep, and my sheep know me. And I will lay down my life for the sheep.

Some sheep I have which are not of this fold; they too must I bring in, and they shall hear my voice, and there shall be one fold, and one shep-herd.

The Jews found fault with his words, and some said, He talks like a mad-man.

As Je-sus went out on the porch at one side of the great church that He-rod built, the Jews came round him and said, How long wilt thou keep us in doubt? If thou be the Christ, tell us so in plain words.

Je-sus said, I told you, and ye had no faith in me. The works that I do, in God's name, are proof that I am sent from him. But ye do not trust me be-cause ye are not my sheep. My sheep hear my voice, and I know them, and they go the way I lead. They shall not be lost, and no one shall take them from me. For God gave them to me, and no one can take them out of his hand. I and my Fa-ther are one.

Then the Jews took up stones to stone him, be-cause he said that he was God.

But he fled from them, and went out of Je-ru-sa-lem to a place near the Jor-dan, where crowds came to hear him, and to be taught of him. And not a few gave their hearts to Je-sus, and sought to lead new lives; to do right and to be good.

**THE LOST SHEEP.**

Ma-ry and Mar-tha, who lived at Beth-a-ny, had a bro-ther whose name was Laz-a-rus, and he was sick. So his sis-ters sent word to Je-sus, but though he was fond of these friends at Beth-a-ny he made no haste to go to them, but staid two days in the place where he was.

Then he said to the twelve, Let us go back to Beth-a-ny, for my friend Laz-a-rus sleeps, and I must go and wake him.

He meant that Laz-a-rus was dead, and that he must go and bring him back to life.

But the twelve thought that he meant that Laz-a-rus slept, as we do when we take our rest.

Now Beth-a-ny was near Je-ru-sa-lem, and a crowd of Jews had gone there to weep with Ma-ry and Mar-tha. As soon as Mar-tha heard that Je-sus was near she ran out to meet him; but Ma-ry sat still in the house. And Mar-tha said to Je-sus, If thou hadst been here my bro-ther would not have died. But I know that e-ven now what thou wilt ask of God he will give it thee.

Je-sus said to her, Thy bro-ther shall rise a-gain.

Mar-tha said, I know that he shall rise at the last day.

Then Mar-tha went back to the house and said to Ma-ry, The mas-ter has come and asks for thee.

Ma-ry rose at once and went out to meet him; and those who saw her leave the house, said, She goes to the grave to weep there.

As soon as Ma-ry came to the place where Je-sus was, she fell at his feet and said, Lord, if thou hadst been here my bro-ther had not died.

When Je-sus saw her tears, and the tears of those who wept with her, he was full of grief, and said, Where have ye laid him?

They said, Lord, come and see.

Je-sus wept. And when the Jews saw it they said, See how he loved him. And some of themsaid, Could not this man, who gave the blind their sight, have saved Laz-a-rus from death?

**LAZ-A-RUS RAISED FROM THE DEAD.**

Je-sus came to the grave. It was a cave, and a stone lay at the mouth of it.

Je-sus said, Take a-way the stone. Mar-tha said to him, By this time he must be in a bad state, for he has been dead four days.

Je-sus said to her, Did I not tell thee that if thou hadst faith thou should see what great things God could do?

Then they took the stone from the place where the dead was laid. And Je-sus cried out with a loud voice, Laz-a-rus, come forth.

And he that was dead came forth, bound hand and foot in his grave clothes, and with his head tied up in a cloth. Je-sus said, Loose him and let him go.

And some of the Jews who came to be with Ma-ry and Mar-tha, and saw this great thing which Je-sus did, had faith in him that he was the son of God. But some of them went to the Phar-i-sees and told what he had done.

And the Phar-i-sees and chief priests met to talk of Je-sus and his deeds. They said it would not do to let him go on in this way, for he would raise up a host of friends who would make him their king. That would not please the Ce-sar of Rome, who would come and take Je-ru-sa-lem from them, and drive the Jews out of the land.

So from that time they sought out some way in which they could put Je-sus to death.

As Je-sus went out of the church where he had taught on the Lord's day, he saw a wo-man all bent up in a heap. She had been so for near a score of years, and could not lift her-self up.

Je-sus said to her, Wo-man, thou art made well. And he laid his hands on her, and she rose at once, and stood up straight, and gave thanks to God.

And the chief man of the church was wroth with Je-sus, be-cause he had done this deed on the day of rest. He said to those in the church, There are six days in which men ought to work; if you want to be cured come then, and not on the day of rest.

Je-sus spoke, and said, Doth not each one of you loose his ox or his ass from the stall and lead him off to drink? And if it is right to do for the ox and the ass what they need, is it not right that this wom-an should be made well on the day of rest?

**THE GREAT SUP-PER.**

And when he said this his foes hung their heads with shame, and all his friends were glad for the great deeds that were done by him.

One Lord's day he went to the house of one of the chief Phar-i-sees, and while there he spoke of a man who made a great feast.

And when it was all spread out, he sent his ser-vant out to bid those come in whom he had asked to the feast.

And they all cried out that they could not come. The first one said, I have bought a piece of ground, and must go and see it; so pray do not look for me.

The next one said, I have bought five yoke of ox-en, and must go and try them; so pray do not look for me.

The next one said, I have just ta-ken a wife, and so can-not come.

So the ser-vant came back to the house and told his mas-ter these things. Then the rich man was in a rage, and he said to his ser-vant, Make haste and go out through the streets and lanes of the town, and bring in the poor, the lame, and the halt and the blind.

And the ser-vant did as he was told. Then he came and said, Lord, I have done as thou didst bid me, and yet there is room for more.

The lord of the house then said, Go out through the high-ways, and down by the hedge-rows, and make the folks come in, that my house may be full; for none of those who were first called shall taste of my feast.

The man who spreads the feast is God. The feast is the good news—that Christ will save us from our sins. The ser-vant means those who preach, and urge men to come to Christ. Those who were first bid to the feast and would not come mean the Jews. And to bid the poor, the lame, and the blind come in-to the feast, means that the poor and the sick are to be saved as well as the rich and the great.

Great crowds drew near to Je-sus, and he told them that though they might come and hear him preach, if they did not care for him in their hearts they were not true friends, and could not be of his band. They must care more for him than for all else in the whole world; and must bear his cross—that is, they must do what is right, as Je-sus did.

# CHAPTER XIV.

## THE PRODIGAL SON.—THE PHARISEE AND THE PUBLICAN.—BABES BROUGHT TO JESUS.—ZACCHEUS CLIMBS A TREE.

JE-SUS said, There was a rich man who had two sons. One of them was wild, and fond of feasts and of gay times, and did not care for his home, or the life that he led there. So he went to his fa-ther and said, Give me, I pray thee, my share of the wealth thou hast laid up for thine heirs, that I may spend it as I choose. And he took his share, and went far from home, and led a gay life.

And when he had spent all he had, there came a dearth in that land, and he was in great want.

That he might not starve, he went out in search of work, and a man hired him, and sent him in the fields to feed swine. And so great was his need of some-thing to eat that he would have been glad to have had some of the coarse food with which the swine were fed, but none of the men gave it to him.

Then he said to him-self, The men my fa-ther hires have more food than they can eat, while I starve for want of what they can well spare. I willrise and go to my fa-ther, and will say to him, Fa-ther, I have done wrong in thy sight, and in the sight of God, and have no more right to be called thy son. Let me come back to thy house, and be as a ser-vant.

So he rose and went to his fa-ther. And while he was yet a long way off his fa-ther saw him, and ran and fell on his neck and kissed him.

And the son said to him, Fa-ther I have done wrong in thy sight, and in the sight of God, and have no more right to be called thy son.

But the fa-ther said to his hired men, Bring forth the best robe and put it on him, and put a ring on his hand, and shoes on his feet. And bring in the fat-ted calf, and kill it, and let us eat and be glad. For this my son was dead, and now lives; he was lost and is found. And tears and sighs gave place to smiles and songs of joy.

## THE PROD-I-GAL'S RE-TURN.

Now the son who had staid at home and kepthis share of wealth that his fa-ther gave him, was at work in the field. And as he came near the house he heard the gay sounds, and called one of the hired men to him and asked what it all meant.

The man said, Thy broth-er is here, and thy fa-ther has made a feast, so great is his joy to have him back safe and sound. And the young man was in a rage, and would not go in the house; so his fa-ther came out and coaxed him.

And he said to his fa-ther, For years and years have I been true to thee and broke none of thy laws. But thou didst not kill a kid for me that I might make a feast for my friends. But as soon as this thy son was come, who spent thy wealth in ways of sin, thou didst kill the fat-ted calf for him.

And the fa-ther said, My son, I have loved thee all thy life, and all that I own is the same as if it was thine; yet it was right that we should be glad and sing songs of joy, for this thy broth-er was dead and now lives; he was lost and is found.

In this way Je-sus taught those who found fault with him, that God was glad to have men turn from their sins and come back to him. He loved them in spite of their sins, and when they made up their minds to leave them, and to do what was right, God met them more than half way, and gave peace and joy to their hearts.

## THE PHAR-I-SEE.

A prod-i-gal is one who wastes all that he has.

Then Je-sus spoke to those who were proud, and felt as if no one else was quite as good as they were. And he said, Two men went up in-to the church to pray. One of them—a Phar-i-see—chose a place where all could see him; and he stood up and said, God I thank thee that I am not like oth-er men. I fast twice a week, and I give to the aid of the church a tenth part of all I own.

But the oth-er man stood far off, and bowed his head, and beat on his breast as he said, God help me, and for-give my sins. And God for-gave thisman more than he did the oth-er, for those that are proud shall be brought low, and those who are meek shall be set in a high place.

Then babes were brought to Je-sus that he might lay his hands on them and bless them. And when the twelve saw it, they tried to keep them back, and would have sent them a-way.

This did not please Je-sus, and he said to them, Let the chil-dren come to me, and do not hold them back, for of such is the king-dom of God.

He meant that no one could have a home with God who was not as good, and sweet, and pure as a young child, who hates sin, and loves God with his whole heart. Then Je-sus took the babes up in his arms, and laid his hands on them, and blest them.

And as he and the twelve went on their way, Je-sus told them that they were to go to Je-ru-sa-lem that those things might be done to him of which the seers and proph-ets spoke. He said that the Jews would beat him and put him to death, but that he should rise from the dead on the third day.

None of the twelve knew what he meant by these things, but thought he would set up his throne on earth, and reign as kings do in this world, and that each one of them would have a place of high rank near his throne.

**"SUF-FER LIT-TLE CHIL-DREN TO COME UN-TO ME."**

When it was known that they were to pass through Jer-i-cho a great crowd came out to meet them. And there was a rich man there who had a great wish to see Je-sus. And his name was Zac-che-us. He was so small that he was quite hid by the crowd, and he was in great fear that Je-sus would pass and he not see him. So he ran on a-head of the crowd; and got up in-to a tree, from whence he could look down at this great man of whom he had heard.

And when Je-sus came to the place he raised his eyes and saw him, and said to him, Zac-che-us, make haste and come down, for to-day I must stay at thy house.

And Zac-che-us came down and went with Je-sus, and was glad to have him as a guest. And there was quite a stir in the crowd, and the Jews found fault with Je-sus, and said that he had gone to be a guest with a man that was full of sin.

But Zac-che-us told Je-sus that if he had done wrong he would do so no more, but would try to be just to all men and to lead a good and pure life.

And when Je-sus saw that he meant what he said, he told Zac-che-us that God would blot out the sins of the past, and help him to lead a new life. For he said that he had come to the world to seek those who had gone wrong, and were like lost sheep, and to save them and bring them to his home in the sky, where there was no such thing as sin or death.

# CHAPTER XV.

## THE FEAST OF THE PASSOVER.—THE SUPPER AT BETHANY.

NOW the great feast of the Pass-o-ver was near, and a great crowd of Jews went up to Je-ru-sa-lem to keep it. It had been kept since the days of Mo-ses, when God smote the first-born of E-gypt, and passed o-ver the homes of the Jews.

And those who were on the watch for Je-sus to do him harm, said, as they stood in the church, What think ye? will he not come to the feast? For the chief priests and Phar-i-sees had sent out word that those who knew where Je-sus was should make it known, that they might take him.

Now six days be-fore the great feast, Je-sus came to Beth-a-ny, where Laz-a-rus was whom he had raised from the dead. Some of the Jews knew that he was there, and they came not so much to see Je-sus as to see Laz-a-rus.

And the chief priests sought for a way to put Laz-a-rus to death, as some of the Jews, when theysaw him had faith in Je-sus, and gave their hearts to him.

Je-sus left Beth-a-ny to go to Je-ru-sa-lem, and on the way the mo-ther of Zeb-e-dee's chil-dren came to Je-sus and begged that he would do one thing for her.

Je-sus said to her, What wilt thou? She said to him, Grant that these my two sons may sit, the one on thy right hand, and the oth-er on thy left, in thy king-dom.

Je-sus said, Ye know not what ye ask. Can ye drink of the cup that I drink of, and bear all that I shall have to bear? They said, We can. Je-sus said, Ye shall drink of the cup, and bear the cross, but to sit on my right hand and on my left is not mine to give; but God gives it to those who are fit for it.

When the ten heard this they were wroth with James and John. But Je-sus told them that those who sought to rule would be made to serve, and that he him-self came not to be served by men but to lay down his life for them.

## CHRIST AND THE MOTH-ER OF ZEB-E-DEE's CHIL-DREN.

And when they came to the Mount of Ol-ives, Je-sus sent two of the twelve, and said to them, Go to the small town which is near you, and you shall find there a colt tied, on which no man has rode. Loose him, and bring him to me, and if you shouldbe asked, Why do ye this? Say that the Lord hath need of him, and he will be sent at once.

**CHIL-DREN IN THE TEM-PLE CRY-ING, "HO-SAN-NA TO THE SON OF DA-VID."**

The men did as Je-sus told them, and brought the young ass and put their robes on his back, and Je-sus sat on him.

And as he went out on the road the crowds on their way to the feast spread their robes be-fore him, and strewed the way with green boughs from the palm trees. And they waved palms in their hands, and made the air ring with shouts of, Ho-san-na to the son of Da-vid! Blest is he that comes in the name of the Lord! Ho-san-na in the high-est!

## THE EN-TRY IN-TO JER-U-SA-LEM.

This was the way in which they used to meet and greet their kings, and they thought to please Je-sus so that he would pay them back when he set up his throne on earth. For the most of them did not love him in their hearts.

As Je-sus came near to Je-ru-sa-lem he looked at it, and wept when he thought of the grief that the Jews were to know.

And he taught each day in the church at Je-ru-sa-lem, but at night he went to Beth-a-ny to sleep.

One morn as he was on his way back to Je-ru-sa-lem he saw a fig-tree by the road-side, and went to it to pluck some of the fruit. But he found on it naught but leaves. Then he said to it, Let no more figs grow on this tree.

The next day when the twelve went by they saw that the fig-tree was dried up from its roots.

And they thought of the words that Je-sus spoke, and said, How soon has the fig-tree dried up!

Je-sus told them that they might do as much and more than he had done to the fig-tree, if they had faith in God, and sought strength from him.

**CHRIST WEEP-ING O-VER JER-U-SA-LEM.**

Then he spoke to them in this way: There was a rich man who laid out a vine-yard, and dug a ditch round it to keep wild beasts and thieves a-way, and made a wine press, and let the place out to men whowere to give him part of the fruit. Then he went off to a far land.

When the time had come for the fruit to be ripe he sent one of his ser-vants to the men who had charge of the vine-yard, that he might bring back his share of the grapes.

But the men took the ser-vant and beat him, and sent him off with no fruit in his hands.

Then the one who owned the place sent once more, and the bad men threw stones at this ser-vant, and hurt him so in the head that he was like to die. The next one they killed, and so things went on.

Now the rich man, who owned the place, had but one son, who was most dear to him. And he said, If I send my son to them they will be kind to him, and treat him well.

But as soon as the bad men saw him they said, This is the heir; let us kill him, and all that is his shall be ours. And they took him and put him to death, and cast him out of the vine-yard.

The vine-yard is the world. The one who owns it is God. The bad men are the Jews; he had taught them his laws, and they had vowed to keep them. When they did not do it, God sent priests and wise men to try and make them do what was right. These were stoned, and not a few were slain.

At last he sent his own dear son, Je-sus. Now they meant to kill him, as the bad men had killed the heir of the vine-yard.

When the Jews heard this talk they knew that Je-sus spoke of them, and they were wroth with him, and in haste to kill him.

One day, on his way out of the tem-ple, Je-sus sat down near the box in which mon-ey was put for the use of the church. And he saw that the rich put in large sums. And there came a poor wid-ow who threw in two mites, which make a far-thing, or the fourth of a pen-ny.

Je-sus said to the twelve, This poor wid-ow has cast in more than all the rest. For they had so much they did not miss what they gave; while she, who was poor and in want, did cast in all that she had.

**THE WID-OW'S MITE.**

# CHAPTER XVI.

## PARABLES.

A par-a-ble is a sto-ry of some-thing in real life that will fix in our minds and hearts the truth it is meant to teach.

Je-sus said the king-dom of heav-en was like the mas-ter of a house who went out at morn to hire men to work in his vine-yard.

The price was fixed at a pen-ny a day, and those who would work for that were sent out to the vine-yard.

At nine o'clock in the day he went out and saw men in the mar-ket place who were out of work, and he said to them, Go ye to the vine-yard, and I will pay you what is right. And they went their way.

He went out at noon, and at three o'clock, and found more men whom he sent to work in his vine-yard. Later in the day, when it was near six o'clock, he went out and saw more men, to whom he said, Why stand ye here all the day i-dle?

They said to him, Be-cause no man has hired us.

**LA-BOR-ERS IN THE VINE-YARD.**

He said, Go ye in-to the vine-yard, and what is right I will give thee.

So when night came, the lord of the vine-yard had the work-men called in, and each one was paid a pen-ny.

When the first came they thought they should have more, and when they were paid but a pen-ny they found fault, and said, These last have wrought but one hour, and thou hast paid them the same as us who have born the toil and heat of the day.

The mas-ter said, Friend, I do thee no wrong. Didst thou not say thou wouldst work for me for a pen-ny a day? Take what is thine, and go thy way; for I have a right to do as I will with mine own. And the last shall be first and the first last.

Je-sus told them a par-a-ble of ten maids who went out to meet the bride-groom. For in those days the man who was wed brought his bride home at night, and some of his friends used to go out to meet him.

These ten maids had lit their lamps, and gone out to meet the bride-groom. But he did not come as soon as they thought he would, and as the hours went on they all fell a-sleep.

Now five of these maids were wise, and five were not. The wise ones had brought oil with them, so that if their lamps should go out they could fill them. Those who were not wise had no oil but that which was in their lamps.

At mid-night those who were on the watch cried out, Lo, the bride-groom comes! Go ye out to meet him.

And the five wise maids rose at once, and went to work to trim their lamps.

The five who were not wise, stood by and said, Give us of your oil, for our lamps have gone out.

But the wise ones said, Not so; for we have no more than we need. Go ye and buy of those who have oil to sell.

And while they went out to buy, the bride-groom came, and those who were in trim went in with him, and the door was shut.

**THE FOOL-ISH VIR-GINS.**

Then the five maids who had been out to buy oil came to the door, and cried out, Lord, Lord, let us in. But he said, I do not know you; and would not let them in.

The bride-groom means Je-sus, who is to come at the last day. The ten maids are those who claim to love him, and who set out to meet him on that day. The oil is the love in our hearts, which burns and keeps our faith bright. We are to watch and wait for him, for we know not the day nor the hour when he will come.

Je-sus came to the town of Beth-a-ny, and they made a sup-per for him there. In those days they did not sit at their meals on chairs as we do, but lay down on a couch, or lounge, as high as the ta-ble, so that they couldrest on the left arm, and have the right hand and arm free to use.

Mar-tha, Ma-ry, and Laz-a-rus were there, and while Je-sus sat at meat Ma-ry came with a flask of rich oil, that was worth a great price. And she broke the flask and poured the oil on the head of Je-sus.

And there were some there who found fault with this great waste, and Ju-das—one of the twelve—said that the oil might have been sold for a large sum that would have done the poor much good.

Je-sus said, Blame her not. She has done a good work on me. For the poor you have with you all the time, and you may do them good when you choose. But you will not have me al-ways.

Then Ju-das went to the chief priests and said, What will you give me if I bring you to the place where Je-sus is, so that you may take him? They said they would pay him well. And from that time he was on the watch to catch Je-sus a-lone.

Je-sus said, There was a rich man, who wore fine clothes, and had great feasts spread for him each day. And a beg-gar named Laz-a-rus lay at his gate, full of sores; but the rich man gave him not so much as a crumb. And the dogs came and licked his sores.

**THE RICH MAN AND THE BEG-GAR.**

The beg-gar died, and was borne by the an-gels to A-bra-ham's bo-som. The rich man died and waslaid in the ground. And while in the pains of hell he raised his eyes and saw A-bra-ham with Laz-a-rus on his bo-som, and he cried and said, Fa-ther A-bra-ham, have mer-cy on me, and send Laz-a-rus that he may dip the tip of his fin-ger in wa-ter and cool my tongue, for this flame tor-ments me.

But A-bra-ham said, Son, thou in thy life-time had thy good things, while Laz-a-rus was poor and had a hard lot. Now he has ease from all his pains and thou art in tor-ments. And be-tween us and you there is a great gulf; none can go from here to you, nor come from you to us.

Then the rich man said, I pray thee then send him to my fa-ther's house, for I have five breth-ren, that he may speak to them, so that they come not to this place of tor-ment.

A-bra-ham said, They have Mo-ses and the proph-ets, let them hear them.

And the rich man said, Nay, fa-ther A-bra-ham; but if one went to them from the dead they will turn from their sins.

And he said to him, If they hear not Mo-ses and the proph-ets they will not turn from their sins though one rose from the dead.

A stew-ard is one who takes charge of a house or lands, pays bills, hires work-men, and is the mas-ter's right-hand man.

Je-sus said, There was a rich man who had a stew-ard. And word was brought to him that this stew-ard made a bad use of his mas-ter's wealth. So the rich man said to him, What is this that I hear of thee? Let me know how thou hast done thy work, if thou wouldst keep thy place.

The stew-ard said to him-self, What shall I do if my lord takes my place from me? I can-not dig, and am too proud to beg. I have made up my mind to do some-thing that will put me on good terms with the rich, so that they will not close their doors to me should I lose my place here as stew-ard.

So he sent for all those who were in debt to his lord. And he said to the first, How much dost thou owe? And he said, A hun-dred mea-sures of oil. The stew-ard said, Take thy bill, and sit down and write fif-ty.

Then said he to the next one, How much dost thou owe? The man said, A hun-dred mea-sures of wheat. The stew-ard said to him, Take thy bill, and write four-score.

## THE UN-JUST STEW-ARD.

And the lord praised the un-just stew-ard, for he thought he had done a wise thing.

Je-sus said we were to use our wealth so as to make friends who will take us in their homes should we be-come poor.

He that is faith-ful in small things is faith-ful al-so in large ones. And he that is un-just in the least, is un-just in much more.

No man can serve two mas-ters.

As Je-sus drew near to Je-ru-sa-lem those who were with him thought that the king-dom he spoke of was close at hand.

He said to them, A rich man had to go to a far land, so he called his ten ser-vants that he might leave his goods in their charge. To the first one he gave five tal-ents. A tal-ent is a large sum in sil-ver. To the next he gave two tal-ents; and to the third one. And he said to them, Make a good use of these gifts till I come back; and then went on his way.

Then he that had five tal-ents went out and bought and sold and made five tal-ents more. And the one that had two did the same. But he that had one dug a hole in the earth and hid his lord's mon-ey.

When the rich man came back he sent for his ser-vants that they might tell him what they had done while he was gone. So he that had had five tal-ents came and said, Lord, thou didst give me five tal-ents, and see—I have gained five more.

His lord said to him, Well done, good and faith-ful ser-vant, thou hast been faith-ful o-ver a few things, I will make thee ru-ler o-ver ma-ny things; en-ter thou in-to the joy of thy lord.

Then he that had two tal-ents came and said, Lord, thou didst give me two tal-ents and I have gained two more.

**THE TAL-ENTS.**

His lord said to him, Well done, good and faith-ful ser-vant, thou hast been faith-ful o-ver a few things, I will make thee ru-ler o-ver ma-ny things; en-ter thou in-to the joy of thy lord.

Then he who had but the one tal-ent came and said, Lord, I knew that thou wert a hard man, and didst reap where thou hast not sown, and gleaned where thou hast not strewn; and, for fear I should lose it, I hid thy tal-ent in the earth, and here it is.

His lord said, Thou wick-ed and la-zy ser-vant, if thou didst know me to be such a harsh man thou shouldst have lent my mo-ney to those who would pay for its use, so that when I came back I should have my own and more with it. Take there-fore the one tal-ent from him and give it to him that hath ten tal-ents. For to him that hath much shall more be giv-en; but from him that hath not, shall be ta-ken a-way all that he hath. And cast ye the use-less ser-vant in-to out-er dark-ness, where shall be weep-ing and gnash-ing of teeth.

Christ meant to teach by this that we were to make use of the gifts or tal-ents that God gave us, and add to them as much as we could. Then when we die God will say to us, Well done, and bid us share in the joy that our lord has in store for us.

If we have but one gift we must use that and serve God with it, or at the last day he will take that from us, and we shall have no part in the joy of our lord.

Je-sus said, The good news is like a king who made a wed-ding feast for his son. And he sent his ser-vants to call in those who were bid to the feast. But they would not come. Then he sent out more ser-vants to urge them to come to the wed-ding. But they made light of it, and went their ways, totheir farms or shops; and some fell on the king's ser-vants and slew them.

**WED-DING GAR-MENT.**

When the king heard of this he was wroth, and he said to his ser-vants, Go ye out to the high-ways and bring in to the wed-ding those ye find there.

And the ser-vants did so, and brought in both bad and good, so there was no lack of guests at the wed-ding.

When the king came in to see the guests, he saw there a man who had not on a wed-ding gar-ment. And he said to him, Friend, why art thou here with-out a wed-ding gar-ment. And the man spoke not.

**LEAV-EN.**

Then said the king to the ser-vants, Bind him hand and foot and take him off, and cast him in-to out-er dark-ness. For ma-ny are called but few are cho-sen.

God is the king who made the feast for Je-sus Christ, his son, to which all are bid. The wed-ding gar-ment we need is a true heart, full of love to Je-sus. The good news is for all, yet those who think more of this world than they do of heav-en, Christ does not choose for his own, and they are lost.

Je-sus said the good news is like un-to leav-en or yeast, which a wo-man took and hid in some meal till the whole of it was light.

# CHAPTER XVII.

## THE LORD'S SUPPER.—JESUS IN GETHSEMANE.—THE JUDAS KISS.—PETER DENIES JESUS.

NOW the day was come when the Jews were to keep the feast of the pass-o-ver. To do this each man took a lamb to the church, and killed it on the al-tar. The priest would burn the fat, but the rest of the lamb the man took home, and it was cooked, and he and his folks ate of it in the night.

The twelve came to Je-sus to ask him at what place they should set out their feast. For they had no house or home of their own.

Je-sus sent forth two of them and said, Go ye to Je-ru-sa-lem, and there shall meet you a man with a jug of wa-ter. Go to the house where he goes, and say to the man who lives there, The mas-ter bids thee show us the room where he shall come to eat the feast with his friends.

And he will show you a large room, up-stairs; there spread the feast.

The men did as Je-sus told them, and the man showed them the room, and there they spread the feast.

And at night Je-sus came with his twelve friends. And as they did eat, Je-sus said, There is one here who will give me up to the Jews.

These words made them all feel sad.

Now there was one of the twelve of whom Je-sus was most fond. His name was John. And as he lay with his head on Je-sus' breast he said to him, Lord, who is it?

Je-sus said, It is he to whom I shall give the piece of bread I dip in the dish.

And when he had dipped the bread he gave it to Ju-das. And he said to him, What is in thy heart to do, do at once.

Now none of the rest knew why Je-sus spoke thus. But as Ju-das had charge of the bag in which the mon-ey was kept, some of them thought that he bade him buy things they were in need of, or give some-thing to the poor. Then Ju-das went out of the house where Je-sus and his friends were; and it was night.

And when he had gone, Je-sus said to them, I shall be with you but a short time. But ere I go a new law I give to you—the law of love. As I have loved you so shall ye love each oth-er. By this shall all men know that ye love me.

Pe-ter said, Lord, where dost thou go?

Je-sus said, Where I go thou canst not come now, but thou shalt be with me by-and-by.

Pe-ter said, Lord, why can-not I go with thee now? I will lay down my life for thy sake!

**PRAY-ING IN THE GAR-DEN.**

Je-sus said, I tell thee, Pe-ter, the cock shall not crow thrice till thou hast sworn thrice that thou dost not know me.

And as they did eat Je-sus took the bread and gave thanks and broke it, and gave to them, and said, Take and eat.

Then he took some wine in a cup, and when he had thanked God, he gave it to them and they all drank of it.

And he told them that when he was dead theymust meet from time to time, and eat the bread and drink the wine in the same way that he had shown them; and as of-ten as they did it they were to think of him, and the death that he died to save men from their sins.

Je-sus spoke with them for some time. Then a hymn was sung and they all went from the house, and came to the Mount of Ol-ives. And they went to a gar-den there, known as Geth-sem-a-ne. And Je-sus took with him Pe-ter, James, and John, and said to them, Sit ye here and watch with me while I go and pray. And he went from them a short way, and knelt down and prayed. And when he thought how soon he was to be put to death for our sins, he was in such grief and pain that the sweat seemed like great drops of blood as it fell to the ground. And God sent an an-gel to calm him and give him strength.

And when he rose from his knees and went back to where his friends were, he found that they slept. And he said to Pe-ter, What, couldst thou not watch with me one hour?

And he went off to pray once more. And when he came back his friends still slept! And he left them and came back a third time. Then he said, Rise up and let us go, for the worst of my foes is close at hand.

**JU-DAS BE-TRAY-ING CHRIST.**

Now Ju-das had been on the watch, and knew when Je-sus went to the gar-den. And as it was dark he thought it would be the best time to give him up to the Jews. So he went to the chief priests and told them, and they sent a band of men out with him to take Je-sus.

Je-sus, who knew all things, knew that Ju-das was near, yet he did not flee.

Ju-das had told the band that he would give them a sign by which they might know which was Je-sus. He said, The one I shall kiss, is he; take him, and hold him fast. Then he came to Je-sus and gave him a kiss.

And the men laid their hands on Je-sus and took him. His friends who were near him said to him, Lord, shall we fight them with the sword?

Pe-ter who had a sword struck one of the band and cut off his ear.

Je-sus said to him, Put thy sword back in its sheath. Could I not pray to God to send me a host of an-gels to fight for me and save me from death? But how then could the words of wise men come true? Then Je-sus touched the man's ear and made it well. And he said to those who took him, Have ye come out with swords and staves as if I were a thief, to take me? I sat from day to day and taught you in the church, and you did not harm me.

Then Pe-ter, James and John, and the rest, were in great fear, and fled from him.

The men that took Je-sus led him off to the house of the high priest, where the scribes and those who had charge of the church had all met.

Pe-ter kept up with the crowd and went in a side door of the house to sit by the fire. And one of the maids of the high priest came to him, and said, Thou wast with Je-sus. But he said, I know not what you mean.

Then he went out on the porch and the cock crew. While there a maid said to those who stood near, This one was with Je-sus.

And Pe-ter said once more that he did not know him. And the cock crew once more.

Now it chanced that one of the high priest's men was a kins-man of the one whose ear Pe-ter had cut off. And he said to him, Did I not see thee in the gar-den with him?

Pe-ter swore that he was not there, and did not know the man. And Je-sus gave him a look as he went by, that was like a stab in Pe-ter's heart. For then the cock crew for the third time, and it came to Pe-ter's mind what Je-sus had said,—Ere the cock crow thrice, thou shalt de-ny me thrice. And he went out and wept as if his heart would break, so great was his grief and shame.

# CHAPTER XVIII.

## CHRIST BEFORE PILATE.—ON THE CROSS.

THE chief court of the Jews met in a room near the church, and was made up of three-score and ten men. The high priest and chief priests were there, and the scribes, and head men of the church, and it was for them to say what should be done to those who broke the laws of Mo-ses; some of whom had to pay fines, or to be shut up in jail. But if a man was to be put to death they had to ask the chief whom the Ce-sar of Rome had set to rule in that part of the land if he would let the deed be done.

It was night when the Jews took Je-sus, and as soon as it was day they brought him in-to court to have him tried. The high priest said to him, Art thou the Christ? tell us.

Je-sus said, If I tell you, ye will not think I speak the truth.

Then they all said, Art thou the son of God?

And he said, I am.

Then the high priest rent his clothes, and said, By his own words we can judge him. What do you say shall be done to him? And they all cried out, Let him be put to death!


Then they spit in his face, and struck Je-sus with the palms of their hands. And they bound him and led him blind-fold to Pi-late's house, and told Pi-late some of the things he had said and done.

Pi-late said to Je-sus, Art thou a king? Je-sus said, I am. But my realm is not of this world, else would my men have fought to set me free.

### "BE-HOLD THE MAN."

Pi-late said, I find no fault with this man. And the Jews were more fierce, and cried that his words had made a great stir in all the land from Gal-i-lee to that place. Pi-late said, if he came from Gal-i-lee they must take him to He-rod, who ruled that part of the land. And He-rod was in Je-ru-sa-lem at that time.

When He-rod saw Je-sus he was glad, for he had heard much of him, and was in hopes to see some great things done by him. But when He-rod spoke to Je-sus, Je-sus said not one word. And the chief priests and scribes stood by, and cried out that he claimed to be king of the Jews, and the son of God, and had taught men that they need not keep the laws of Mo-ses or of Rome. These were crimes for which he ought to be put to death.

So He-rod and his men of war made sport of Je-sus, and put on him a robe such as kings wear; for he had said he was a king. And then He-rod sent him back to Pi-late.

Pi-late said, I find no fault in this man; nor does He-rod, for I sent you to him; he had done naught for which he should be put to death.

Now it was the rule when this great feast was held, that one of those who were shut up in jail should be set free. And at this time there was a Jew there, whose name was Ba-rab-bas; and he had killed some one.

Pi-late said, Which one shall I set free—Ba-rab-bas, or Je-sus, who is called Christ?

**PI-LATE WASH-ING HIS HANDS.**

While Pi-late spoke, his wife sent word to him to do no harm to that just man, for she had had a strange dream a-bout him. But the chief priests urged the mob to ask that Ba-rab-bas be set free.

Pi-late said, What then shall I do with Je-sus, who is called Christ?

They cried out, Hang him! Hang him!

When Pi-late saw that he could not get them to ask for Je-sus, he took some wa-ter and washed his hands in full view of the mob, and said, I am not to blame for the death of this just man; see ye to it.

Then the Jews said, Let his blood be on us and on our chil-dren.

But Pi-late was to blame for Je-sus' death; for he gave him up to the Jews that he might please them, and keep the place that he had.

Now it was the law of the land that a man should be scourged ere he was hung. So Je-sus was stripped to the waist, and his hands were bound to a low post in front of him so as to make him stoop, and while he stood in this way he was struck with rods, or a whip of cords, till the blood burst through the skin.

**BE-HOLD THE MAN.**

Then Pi-late's men of war led him to a room, and took off his own robe, and put on him one of a red and blue tint. Then they made a crown of thorns and put it on his head; and they put a reed in his right hand. Then they bowed down to him, as if he were a king, and mocked at him and said, Hail, King of the Jews! And they spat on him, and took the reed and struck him on the head, and smote him with their hands.

When Ju-das saw that Je-sus was to be put to death, he was in great grief to think he had brought such a fate on one who had done no wrong. And he took back to the chief priests the sum they had paid him, and he said to them, I have done a great sin to give up to you one who had done no wrong. They said to him, What is that to us? See thou to that. Then Ju-das threw down the sil-ver, and went out and hung him-self.

Then the men of war took off the gay robe from Je-sus, and put his own clothes on him and led him out to put him to death.

They met a man named Si-mon, and made him bear the cross. And a great crowd of men and wo-men went with them who wept and mourned for Je-sus. Je-sus told them not to weep for him, but for them-selves and their chil-dren, be-cause of the woes that were to come on the Jews.

They brought him to a place called Cal-va-ry, not far from the gates of Je-ru-sa-lem. And they nailed his feet and hands to the cross, which was then set up in the ground. And all the while Je-sus prayed, Fa-ther for-give them, for they know not what they do. He meant that they did not know how great was their sin; nor that they had in truth put to death the son of God. With him they hung two thieves, one on his right hand, and one on his left.

**CHRIST CAR-RY-ING HIS CROSS.CHRIST CAR-RY-ING HIS CROSS.**

Then they sat down to watch Je-sus, who hung for hours on the cross in great pain, ere his death came to him. And they took his robes and gave each one a share; but for his coat they cast lots. Andat the top of the cross Pi-late had put up these words:

JE-SUS OF NAZ-A-RETH, KING OF THE JEWS.

And the Jews as they went by shook their heads at him, and said, If thou be the son of God come down from the cross, and the chief priests and the scribes mocked him and said, His trust was in God; let God save him now if he will have him.

**CHRIST ON CAL-VA-RY.**

One of the thieves spoke to Je-sus and said, If thou art the Christ save thy-self and us.

But the oth-er said, Dost thou not fear God when thou art so soon to die? It is right that we should die for our sins, but this man has done no wrong. And he said to Je-sus, Think of me when thou art on thy throne. Je-sus said to him, This day shalt thou be with me where God is.

**THE CRU-CI-FIX-ION.**

Now there stood near the cross of Je-sus his mo-ther, and John—the one of the twelve most dear to him. And he bade John take care of his mo-ther, and told her to look on John as her son. And John took her to his own home to take care of her and give her all that she had need of.

From the sixth to the ninth hour—that is, from twelve to three o'clock—the sky was dark in all the land. And Je-sus thought that God had turned his face from him. And he cried out with a loud voice O God! O God! why hast thou left me?

One of the men near thought he was in pain, and he took a sponge and dipped it in the gall, and put it up on a reed to his mouth, so that Je-sus might drink. Je-sus wet his lips with the drink that was to ease his pain, then spoke once more, bowed his head and died.

Then the veil which hung in the church, in front of the ark, was torn in two; the earth shook; the rocks were split; the graves gave up their dead, and those who, while they lived, had served the Lord, rose and came out of their graves and went in-to Je-ru-sa-lem and were seen there.

When those who had kept watch of Je-sus as he hung on the cross, saw these things that were done, they were in great fear, and said, There is no doubt that this man was the son of God.

**LAY-ING IN THE TOMB.**

As night came on the Jews went to Pi-late and begged him to kill Je-sus and the two thieves so that they could be put in their graves. For it would not do for them to hang on the cross on the day of rest. The men on guard broke the legs of the thieves to kill them, and thrust a spear in-to Je-sus' side to make sure that he was dead.

Now there was near Cal-va-ry a gar-den, in which was a tomb in which no one had been laid. It was cut in a rock, and was owned by a rich man—Jo-seph of Ar-i-ma-the-a. He came to Pi-late and begged that he might lay Je-sus in this grave, and Pi-late told him to do so. And Jo-seph took Je-sus down from the cross, and wrapped him in the fine lin-en he had brought, and laid him in the tomb, and put a great stone at the door, and left him there.

**DEATH OF SAP-PHI-RA.**

The chief priests went to Pi-late and said, It has come to our minds that Je-sus said that he would rise on the third day, so we pray thee to have men watch the tomb lest some of his friends come and steal him, and then go and say that he rose from the dead.

Pi-late said, Ye have your own watch-men. Go and make it as sure as you can.

So they went and put a seal of wax on the great tomb, and set men to watch by the tomb.

But that night God sent down an an-gel, and he came and rolled back the stone from the door, and sat on it. His face shone like fire, and his robes were white as snow. And the watch-men shook for fear of him, and had no more strength than dead men.

# CHAPTER XIX.

## JESUS LEAVES THE GRAVE.—APPEARS TO MARY.—STEPHEN STONED.—PAUL'S LIFE, AND DEATH.

ON the first day of the week, as soon as it was light, three wo-men, friends of Je-sus, came to the tomb with the gums and spice they used to lay out their dead.

And they said as they went, Who shall roll the stone a-way from the door of the tomb?

And lo, when they came near they found that the great stone had been rolled a-way. And when they went in the tomb, they saw an an-gel clothed in a long white robe, and they shook with fear.

He said to them, Have no fear. Ye seek Je-sus, who was put to death on the cross. He is not here, though this is the place where they laid him. Go tell his friends that he has ris-en from the dead, and bid them go to Gal-i-lee where they shall see him.

Two of the wo-men from the tomb, with fear and yet with joy, ran to tell the good news.

But Ma-ry Mag-da-le-ne stood out-side the tomb and wept. And as she stooped down and looked in the tomb, she saw two an-gels in white, the one at the head, the oth-er at the foot of the place where Je-sus had lain.

And they said to her, Why dost thou weep? She said, Be-cause they have ta-ken my Lord a-way, and I know not where they have laid him. And when she had thus said, she drew back and saw that Je-sus stood near, yet knew not that it was he.

Je-sus said to her, Ma-ry! She turned and said to him, Mas-ter!

Je-sus said, Touch me not, for I have not yet gone up to my Fa-ther; but go tell the breth-ren what thou hast seen and heard.

And Ma-ry told them that she had seen the Lord, and all that he had said to her.

And Je-sus was seen two or three times on the earth af-ter his death, and he came and spoke to those who were to teach and preach as he had taught them. But Thom-as was not with the rest when the Lord came. And when they told him that they had seen the Lord, he said, I doubt it. But if I shall see in his hands the marks of the nails, and thrust my hand in the wound the spear made in his side, then shall I know that it is he.

**HE IS RIS-EN.**

In eight days these friends met in a room to talk a

nd pray. Thom-as was with them and the door was shut. Then came Je-sus and stood in theirmidst and said, Peace be un-to you. Then said he to Thom-as, Reach here and touch my hands, and put thy hand in my side, and doubt no more that I have ris-en from the dead.

When Thom-as heard his voice and knew that it was Je-sus, he said, My Lord and my God. Je-sus said to him, Thom-as, be-cause thou hast seen me, thou hast faith in me; blest are they that have not seen me, and yet put their trust in me.

At the end of five weeks he met with these friends at Je-ru-sa-lem. And when he had had a talk with them he led them out as far as Beth-a-ny. And he raised his hands and blest them, and as he stood thus he went up in a cloud out of their sight.

When the day of Pen-te-cost, or har-vest feast, had come, Pe-ter, and the rest of those whom Je-sus had taught, were all in one place.

And all at once there came the great rush of a strong wind that filled the room where they were. And tongues of fire came down on each one of them, and their hearts were filled with a strange pow-er, and they spoke all known tongues.

And there were men there from all parts of the East, and when they heard these men of Gal-i-lee speak in their own tongues of the works of God, they were in a maze. And some said, These men are full of new wine.

**CHRIST AP-PEAR-ING TO MA-RY.**

But Pe-ter stood up and said the men were not drunk, but that this strange gift of speech was one of the signs that God had told the Jews that he would send on the earth. And Pe-ter preached so well to the crowd that not a few left the ranks of sin and gave their hearts to Christ, and to good works.

From that time those who had been in the school in which Je-sus taught while on earth went out to teach and preach the good news. They gave alms to the poor, healed the sick, and did all the good that they could.

One of them, named Ste-phen, stood up to preach and to tell the Jews what God had done for them, and to try to make them give up their sins. He spoke in plain words, and said, The Jews of old put to death those who were sent to tell them that Je-sus was to come; and now you have slain the Just One him-self.

When the Jews heard this they were full of rage, and gnashed their teeth at him like wild beasts. But he raised his eyes to the sky, and saw a great light there. And he said, I see Je-sus on the right hand of God.

Then they cried out with a loud voice, and stopped their ears so that they could not hear his words; and they brought him out of the town, and stoned him.

**THE AS-CEN-SION TO HEAV-EN.**

And Ste-phen knelt down, and asked God to for-give them for this sin. And then he died.

The men who threw the stones at Ste-phen took off their cloaks, that they might have the free use of their arms, and laid them at the feet of a young man named Saul.

**HOU-SES ON THE WALLS OF DA-MAS-CUS.**

Now Saul had done much harm to the good cause, and was in a great rage with those who were friends of Je-sus and taught his truths. So he went to the high priest at Je-ru-sa-lem and asked to be sent to Da-mas-cus, that if he found friends of Je-sus there he might bind them with cords and bring them backto Je-ru-sa-lem. And the high priest gave him notes to those who had charge of the church-es in Da-mas-cus, and he set out for that place. But when he came near the town there shone round him a great light, and he was in such fear that he fell to the ground. And a voice said to him, Saul, Saul, why dost thou hate me and hunt me down?

**THE COM-ING OF THE HO-LY GHOST.**

Saul said, Who art thou, Lord? The voice said, I am Je-sus, whom thou dost use so ill.

Then Saul shook with fear and said, Lord, what wilt thou have me to do? The Lord said, Rise, and go in-to the town, and it shall be shown thee what thou must do. And the men who were with him stood dazed and dumb, for they heard the voice, but could see no man.

When Saul rose from the earth he could not see, for the light had made him blind; and those who were with him led him by the hand in-to Da-mas-cus. And for three days he had no sight; and he could not eat nor drink.

But God sent An-a-ni-as, a good man, to touch his eyes, and his sight and his strength came back. And his heart was changed, and there was no man who could preach as Paul did, by which name he was now known.

For a while he went with Bar-na-bas. Then he took Si-las with him, and they made both friends andfoes. The Jews at Phil-ip-pi found fault with them, beat them and put them in jail, and bade the jail-er keep them safe. So he made their feet fast in the stocks—which were great blocks of wood with holes in them.

At mid-night Paul and Si-las prayed, and those in the jail heard them. Then all at once there came a great earth-quake which shook the jail, and the doors flew o-pen, and the chains fell from those who were bound. The jail-er woke from his sleep, and when he saw that not a door was shut, he feared he would be put to death if those in the jail had fled. So he drew his sword to kill him-self. But Paul cried to him with a loud voice, Do thy-self no harm, for we are all here.

**THE CON-VER-SION OF ST. PAUL.**

Then the jail-er brought a light, and came to the cell where Paul and Si-las were, and he knelt there, and cried out, Sirs, what must I do to be saved? And they said, Have faith in the Lord Je-sus Christ, and thou shalt be saved.

That same hour of the night the jail-er took Paul and Si-las and washed their wounds, and brought them food, and his heart was full of joy, for he and all in his house were made Chris-tians, and God would for-give their past sins.

The next morn the chief men at Phil-ip-pi sent word to the jail-er to let those men go, for the Jews found they had no right to beat Paul. And they feared the law, and begged him to leave the town.

Paul went to A-thens, the chief town of Greece, which was full of false gods, to whom al-tars had been built. But there was one al-tar on which were the words, TO THE UN-KNOWN GOD.

Those who built it felt that there was one God of whom they had not been taught, and this al-tar was for him.

Paul taught in A-thens, both in-doors and out-doors. And when the wise men heard that he told of Je-sus, and that we were all to rise from the dead, they brought him to Mars' Hill, where the chief court was held. And they said to him, Tell us now what the good news is. For thou dost speak strange words, and we would like to know what they mean.

**ST. PAUL LEAV-ING TYRE.**

Paul told them there was but one true God, andthey must serve him and give up their sins, and put their trust in Je-sus, and they would all be saved at the last day.

Then Paul went to Co-rinth, where he spent some time. At the end of some years he came back to Je-ru-sa-lem. And the Lord's friends met him, and were glad to see his face once more. And he told them where he had been, and how God had helped him.

And Paul went up to the church. And while he was there some Jews from A-si-a saw him and took hold of him, and cried out, Men of Is-ra-el, help us. This is the man who has taught that we werenot to do as Mo-ses told us, nor to come here to pay our vows. And he has brought with him Gen-tiles whom it is a crime to let come in-to our church.

Soon all the town was in an up-roar, and Paul was brought in-to the church, and the gates that led to the courts were all shut. As they were a-bout to kill him, some one went and told the chief who had charge of a band of Ro-man troops, and dwelt near the great church to guard it. And he and some of his men ran down in the midst of the crowd, who, as soon as they saw them, ceased to beat Paul.

The chief took Paul from them, and had him bound with chains, and asked who he was and what he had done. Some cried this, and some that, and no one could tell just what they said.

And the chief led him off to his own house, to save Paul's life, and the mob brought up the rear, and cried out, A-way with him! Kill him! The next day the chief let Paul go, and sent him to Fe-lix, who ruled in Ju-de-a. And here he was shut up in jail, and was there for two years or more. He told them who he was, and why he had gone to Je-ru-sa-lem, and said he had done no wrong that he knew of; though some might say it was wrong for him to preach that the dead should rise from their graves at the last day.

**ST. PAUL PREACH-ING AT A-THENS.**

Fe-lix sent the Jews off, and bade the jail-er let Paul walk in and out as he chose, and see all the friends who might call. He was there for two years, and at the end of that time Fes-tus took Fe-lix's place.

At last he was sent to Rome to be tried be-fore the Ce-sar. While on the sea a fierce wind sprang up, and beat the ship so that the men could not steer. And they were in great fear lest they should drown. But Paul told them not to fear, for though the ship might be a wreck there would be no loss of life. At the end of two weeks the ship struck the isle of Mal-ta, and the men swam to the shore on bits of boards.

ST. PAUL'S SHIP-WRECK.

**MEET-ING PLACE IN A-THENS.**

Paul staid here for three months, and then went to Rome, where he dwelt for two years or more, and taught men to trust in the Lord and to do right.

We are not told when or how he died.

# CHAPTER XX.

## WHAT JOHN SAW WHILE ON THE ISLE OF PATMOS.—THE GREAT WHITE THRONE.—THE LAND OF LIGHT.

JOHN wrote the last book in the New Tes-ta-ment. It is called Rev-e-la-tion; and that means that it tells what no one else but John knew.

John was sent to the lone isle of Pat-mos by one of the bad Em-pe-rors of Rome, who would not let him preach or teach the truths that Christ taught.

While he was at Pat-mos Je-sus came to him in a dream, and showed him all the things that he wrote of in this book.

John says: I heard a great voice like a trum-pet, and as I turned to see who it was that spoke to me, I saw Je-sus clothed in a robe that fell to his feet, and was held at the waist by a belt of gold. And when I saw him I fell at his feet like one dead. And he laid his right hand on me, and said, Fear not; I am he who died on the cross, but who now lives to die no more.

**PAT-MOS.**

Je-sus told John to write down all that he saw, and to send it to the church-es for which it was meant.

Then John saw a door o-pen in the sky, and a voice said to him, Come up here, and I will show thee what will take place in the time to come. And he heard the an-gels sing songs of praise to Je-sus, whom they called the Lamb that was slain. And John was shown strange things that were to teach him what the friends of Christ would have to put up with till the end of the world. And he was shown, too, how the Lord would save them from their foes, so that at last no one could hurt or harm them.

Then John saw a great white throne in heav-en, and Je-sus sat on it. And the dead rose from their graves, and came and stood near the throne to be judged. All the things that they had done while on the earth were put down in the books out of which they were judged. And if their names were not in the Book of Life they were cast in-to the lake of fire.

When this great day was past, John saw new skies and a new earth, for the old earth and skies had been burnt up, And he saw the New Je-ru-sa-lem come down from the skies, and heard a voice say that God would come and live with men.

Round the New Je-ru-sa-lem, which was built of gold, was a high wall with twelve gates, three on each side. At each gate was an an-gel to guard it. In the walls were all kinds of rich and rare gems, and its twelve gates were made of pearls.

There was no need of the sun or the moon, for God was there and Je-sus, and they made it light. And those whom Je-sus had saved—Jews and Gen-tiles, rich and poor—were to come and live in it. And the gates should not be shut, for there will be no night there. And none but those whose names are in the Book of Life shall go in-to it.

And John saw a pure riv-er called the wa-ter of life. On each side of it grew the tree of life that bore twelve kinds of fruit, which were ripe each month. And those who dwell in that land of light, and eat the fruits of the tree of life, and drink of the wa-ter of life, shall see the Lord's face and be with him and serve him.

He will wipe all tears from their eyes, and there shall be no more death, nor grief, nor pain.

Je-sus said to John, Blest are they who keep God's laws and do his will, that they may pass through the gates to his bright home on high.

**THE END.**